W9-BVI-978

LINCOLN'S LAST TRIAL

THE MURDER CASE THAT PROPELLED HIM TO THE PRESIDENCY

YOUNG READERS' EDITION

LINCOLN'S LAST TRIAL

THE MURDER CASE THAT PROPELLED HIM TO THE PRESIDENCY

YOUNG READERS' EDITION

DAN ABRAMS

AND DAVID FISHER

HANOVER
SQUARE
PRESS

ISBN-13: 978-1-335-91785-0

Lincoln's Last Trial: The Murder Case That Propelled Him to the Presidency

Young Readers' Edition

Library of Congress Cataloging-in-Publication Data has been applied for.

HanoverSqPress.com
BookClubbish.com

Printed in U.S.A.

I dedicate this book to my mentor and father, Floyd Abrams, whose genuine love for, and mastery of, history and the law established a lifelong example that I continue to emulate, but will never quite live up to.

TABLE OF CONTENTS

A Note from the Author 9
Introduction 15
Chapter One 21
Chapter Two 28
Chapter Three 33
Chapter Four 41
Chapter Five 50
Chapter Six 56
Chapter Seven 63
Chapter Eight 70
Chapter Nine 76
Chapter Ten 84
Chapter Eleven 90
Chapter Twelve 96
Chapter Thirteen 102
Chapter Fourteen 108
Chapter Fifteen 115
Chapter Sixteen 123
Chapter Seventeen 130

Chapter Eighteen 138
Chapter Nineteen 145
Chapter Twenty 152
Chapter Twenty-One 157
Chapter Twenty-Two 161
Chapter Twenty-Three 168
Chapter Twenty-Four 176
Chapter Twenty-Five 182
Chapter Twenty-Six 190
Chapter Twenty-Seven 201
Chapter Twenty-Eight 206
Epilogue 214
Glossary 223
Acknowledgments 229

A NOTE FROM THE AUTHOR

I work as a lawyer, and a lot of what I do is report for television on some of the most famous legal cases of our times. For me, the best cases are the close ones. They are the ones where the verdict is uncertain. They are the ones where each day's testimony and lawyering [the work of the lawyers on the case] have the potential to change the case's outcome by changing the jury's mind.

I am also a history buff. I've had a great interest in history ever since I was a student. Now I find it rewarding to have a book or e-reader in hand every night before bed to do some reading on my favorite subjects, including World Wars I and II, the history of the law, and the lives of US presidents.

Before he became president in 1860, our country's sixteenth president, Abraham Lincoln, worked as a lawyer. His very last murder trial as a lawyer took place in 1859. Stenographer Robert Roberts Hitt was hired to write a transcript of the trial. Today, it is standard practice for there to be a written record, called a transcript, of everything that is said during a trial. It is the job of a court stenographer to make that record. But in 1859, most trials just had summaries written about them. Very few trials had detailed, word-for-word transcripts. For those trials that did, stenographers like Hitt would dip their steel-tipped pens in inkwells and hurry to write down on paper everything as it was being said.

In 1989, Hitt's original transcript, nearly one hundred handwritten pages, was found in perfect condition in a garage in California! I remember being struck by how limited the news coverage was about this important document being discovered. After all, it *was* one of the final trials of Abraham Lincoln's career. And it wasn't just any trial, it was a murder case.

The State of Illinois versus Simeon "Peachy" Quinn Harrison was one of the most famous trials of its time. Lincoln had been hired to defend Harrison, a young man who had stabbed another young man to death.

But was it self-defense or not? How Lincoln and the defense team presented their case *for* Harrison and how the prosecution presented their case *against* Harrison would have an impact on the verdict. It was one of those close cases where lawyering could make all the difference. And one of those lawyers, Abraham Lincoln, was a man not only known for his excellent public speaking skills, but he was also a rising political star at the time.

The Peachy Quinn Harrison trial took place just nine months before the convention to nominate a Republican candidate for president. Lincoln's name was being bandied about as a potential choice for the nomination. There was a lot of public attention on him. If he made any sort of mistake in his work as a lawyer right now, it might hurt his chances at the convention. By taking this difficult case, Lincoln seemed to have far more to lose than gain.

I believe, by the way, that this case and trial would have been considered newsworthy by today's standards even if Lincoln had not been a part of it. Harrison and the man he stabbed to death, Greek Crafton, had known each other for years. One of the eyewitnesses was Crafton's own brother. Another witness was a celebrity at the time. There was also a lot to be said about who was standing exactly where and doing exactly what when. There was an alleged deathbed admission by Crafton, too. The people of Springfield, Illinois, where the murder and trial look place, knew both Harrison and Crafton. Many people held strong opinions one way or the other, and the community was fiercely divided.

In order to tell this story properly we needed to truly understand the context of the trial itself. For that, we conducted an enormous amount of legal and historical research beyond the courtroom. This included a thorough examination of how this case compared with others Lincoln argued during his law career. And so, this book is also able to present a peek at the early history of law in America, including the laws on hearsay and on self-defense. The law of self-defense in 1859, it turns out, was not that different from how it is in most states today.

This is, in the end, a story about a great lawyer trying a difficult case in the town where he lived. Every aspect of and detail in this story is rooted solidly in fact. The participants in the trial and the dialogue from it are real. Every quotation comes directly from Hitt's transcript. It is because of Hitt's fine work that we know exactly what happened in the courtroom every day. That is why much of this book is told from Hitt's point of view.

The information, history, and law presented are entirely accurate. Newspaper reporting from the time assisted with detailed descriptions of the trial beyond exactly what was said in court, about everything from the weather to the reactions from the gallery. And a host of books about Lincoln provided additional information and perspective on Lincoln the lawyer.

James M. Cornelius, the curator of the Lincoln collection at Springfield's Abraham Lincoln Presidential Library and Museum, reviewed the manuscript of this book for accuracy.

With that said, there were times we had to figure out what was most likely said in meetings or private conversations or suggest appropriate thoughts or mannerisms. We kept any re-created quotes from Lincoln himself to an absolute minimum, in part because there is so much information about him readily available, and even then we have been careful to base those quotes on his previously stated beliefs as well as known conversations. We also made certain minor assumptions on the timing of the trial where the historical record was unclear.

This is, at its core, for me, an exciting trial that pairs my favorite kind of legal case with my fascination with history. I am pleased to be the one to share Lincoln's last trial with you.

INTRODUCTION

By 1859, the United States was rushing headlong into its golden future. Oregon was admitted to the Union as the thirty-third state. In June, the Comstock silver lode was discovered in Nevada, and the great silver rush began. In July, Amherst beat Williams in the first intercollegiate baseball game, and daring balloonists set a distance record that would stand until the end of the century. They flew 809 miles from St. Louis, Missouri, to Henderson, New York. In early August, Otis Tuft received a patent for the first passenger elevator. Weeks later, America's first oil well was drilled near Titusville, Pennsylvania, marking the beginning of the oil rush.

But the foundation of it all had been built on shaky ground.

One issue, slavery, divided the country like no other. The moral issues of slavery were obvious. But getting out of it was so complicated. The economy of the South had grown dependent on it. Its abrupt elimination would cause widespread devastation throughout that region. People wanted easy answers and there were none.

Then, in 1857, the Supreme Court ruled that slaves, former slaves, and their descendants could not become United States citizens. The Supreme Court also ruled that Congress did not have the right to prohibit the expansion of slavery into US territories. In response, the antislavery movement grew rapidly. Abolitionists in the North began funding those who were in favor of an armed uprising.

At the same time, fearing the end of slavery, the South was openly discussing secession from the Union. The word *war* was being tossed around as if it had no cost.

Americans were beginning to accept the reality that the young nation could not move forward until the question of slavery was resolved once and for all. While some in the Republican Party demanded the end of slavery, there were many differing opinions about how this might be achieved. These positions ranged from outlawing slavery immediately, by force, if necessary, to prohibiting its expansion into new states and territories and allowing it to eventually die out.

In June 1858, Abraham Lincoln received and accepted the Republican nomination for the senate from Illinois. In his now-famous acceptance speech, he addressed the issue of slavery. He stated that the entire nation must decide for or against it.

"A house divided against itself cannot stand," he said. "I believe this government cannot endure, permanently half slave and half free. I do not expect the Union to be dissolved—I do not expect the house to fall—but I do expect it will cease to be divided. It will become all one thing or all the other. Either the opponents of slavery will arrest the further spread of it, and place it where the public mind shall rest in the belief that it is in the course of ultimate extinction, or its advocates will push it forward, till it shall become alike lawful in all the States, old as well as new—North as well as South."

Lincoln had tried to keep his own personal beliefs out of this and other political speeches. He sincerely hoped that there might be some way to lawfully end this inhuman practice.

Lincoln lost the 1858 election to Stephen Douglas and continued to practice law. By September 1859 he was considered a long-shot candidate for the Republican nomination for president the following year. New York senator William H. Seward was the favorite. Ohio governor Salmon Chase, Pennsylvania senator Simon Cameron, and former Missouri congressman Edward Bates each had their supporters.

For Lincoln, the best strategy was to allow these other candidates to remain the focus. He knew that in this divided country any candidate's firm stand would turn away voters.

Meanwhile, Lincoln continued to polish his image as a man of the people, as a brilliant lawyer defending not simply his clients, but the virtues of the law itself.

After more than twenty years, this self-taught lawyer had risen to the top of the legal profession. Before he began any trial, Lincoln prepared himself thoroughly. He took the jumbled facts of a case and sorted through them, trying to put them in order and determine where to make his stand. An important aspect of that meant thoroughly assessing the case against him and his client. He once said that he always studied the opposite side of every disputed question, every law case, and every political issue, more thoroughly, if possible, than his own side. As a result, in all his long practice, he had never once been surprised in court by the strength of his adversary's case. Instead, he often found it much weaker than he had initially feared.

Lincoln's courtroom appearances drew large crowds that hung on to his words. His stirring use of everyday language allowed him to forge a remarkable connection with his audience. People simply liked him. They liked his folksy approach and his slightly disheveled appearance. Lincoln reasoned with witnesses calmly and treated the jury with respect, and so they believed him.

Lincoln built a personal relationship between himself and the jury. It was a relationship strong enough that it required a mountain of evidence to overcome his claim that his client was innocent. This was his gift: by the end of a trial, the jury just didn't want to let him down.

Lincoln had become especially famous for the power of his closing arguments. He possessed the rare ability to move juries in their minds and hearts by weaving facts and emotions into a believable tale. And there was no time limit on the length of a summation, which served Lincoln well. He was never in a hurry when justice was at stake.

In Springfield, Illinois, the first week of September in 1859, Lincoln brought all his experience and skills to bear on his twenty-seventh and final murder trial. And for just a short while, people set aside the problems of the world and the nation as the trial of Peachy Quinn Harrison for the murder of Greek Crafton captured their attention.

1

Robert Roberts Hitt, the well-known stenographer, arrived in Springfield, Illinois, late on the sweltering afternoon of August 28, 1859. As he stepped down onto the platform of the new train station, he paused briefly. He patted the beads of sweat on his forehead, then attempted, unsuccessfully, to tug the wrinkles out of his jacket. The Alton Express had traveled the two hundred miles from Chicago in just nine hours.

Hitt had tried with limited success to practice his shorthand on the ever-shaking rails. It had not surprised him that the train was far more crowded than

"THE HONORABLE R.R. HITT, ILLINOIS," HALFTONE PRINT OF A DRAWING, GEORGE WILLIAM BRECK, *HARPER'S WEEKLY*, MAY 5, 1894, COLLECTION OF THE US HOUSE OF REPRESENTATIVES

This drawing of Robert Roberts Hitt appeared in Harper's Weekly *magazine in 1894, many years after he wrote the transcript for Lincoln's last murder trial.*

he had previously experienced. Many of his fellow passengers had the same destination in Springfield that he did. They were going to attend the Simeon "Peachy" Quinn Harrison murder trial.

Hitt had been hired to be the stenographer for the trial. He was going to be present in the courtroom and write down everything that was said. He would create a transcript, a word-for-word record of the trial. This trial had been attracting a lot of attention once it became known that the lawyer Abraham Lincoln was going to defend the accused killer.

The previous fall, Lincoln had run against Stephen Douglas to become senator from Illinois. Lincoln lost the election, but during the campaign he and Douglas had seven debates. These debates gained Lincoln a national reputation. Some people were predicting he was going to make a run for the presidency in 1860. There was great interest in the man, and all the newspapers in the area were covering the trial, including the *Chicago Press and Tribune*. The country had been introduced to Lincoln. Thus far, people liked what they saw, and they wanted to see more of him at the upcoming murder trial.

Hitt already knew a lot about Lincoln. Although he dismissed it humbly when offered credit, it was Hitt's own fine work that had helped bring Lincoln to the public's attention. As a student at the Rock River Seminary and at DePauw University, Hitt had taken a keen interest in phonography, the skill of rapidly converting spoken words to print. Hitt became quite an expert at this form of shorthand. It was a well-paying trade, and he opened his own office in Chicago in 1856. He worked regularly for the state legislature, the courts, and, on occasion, for newspapers, which were rapidly adopting this new form of journalism.

Hitt had first met Abe Lincoln in 1857. Hitt had been hired by the *Chicago Daily Press* to cover the Effie Afton trial. In that case Lincoln defended a railroad from land claims he considered unjust. During the trial Lincoln had taken a liking to Hitt, who he viewed as an energetic young reporter.

A great stir was created when Lincoln and Douglas announced they would debate the complex moral, legal, and economic issues of slavery and state's rights. *Chicago Press and Tribune* co-owner and managing editor Joseph Medill hired Hitt to bring a word-for-word account of the debates to his readers. Hitt's transcriptions attracted a lot of attention. To be able to read in the morning paper a speech that had been given just the night before was a new and wonderful thing.

Hitt's transcriptions of the debates were sent by telegraph to newspapers throughout the entire country, including Horace Greeley's important *New York Tribune*. In just a few weeks Lincoln went from being a little-known Illinois lawyer to a widely admired political figure.

Lincoln was so taken with these transcripts that he requested and bought two copies from the newspapers and later published them as a book. The book sold more than thirty thousand copies.

Lincoln spoke plainly and forcefully, and the power

of his words defined his character for many thousands of Americans. But he also was sharp enough to realize that Hitt's work could add value to his ambitions. In fact, Lincoln refused to begin the second debate until Hitt was taken out of the crowd and seated up on the stage with the debaters.

The two men, the tall, angular Lincoln and the small, slender Hitt, became good friends. Now this murder trial would bring them together again. Lincoln had already agreed to defend Harrison when Hitt was hired by the *Illinois State Journal* to provide a daily transcript for its readers.

Hitt was quite pleased to accept this opportunity. In addition to his substantial fees, the attention given to the trial would surely boost his own growing reputation in his field. Trial transcriptions were still extremely rare. There were no devices to assist the reporter. Every word had to be captured by hand. It was an extraordinarily time-consuming and difficult process. Especially in a courtroom where complicated legal terms and phrases were used so often. In most trials, there didn't seem to be much need for every word to be written down. Judges didn't rely on transcripts to make their decisions. Summaries of the proceedings were much more common. And when necessary, lawyers were expected to be truthful in their memories.

ABRAHAM LINCOLN PRESIDENTIAL LIBRARY AND MUSEUM

This photograph of Abraham Lincoln was taken in early October 1859, a month after his last murder trial as a lawyer ended.

However, there were those who saw the value in a word-for-word transcript. After this trial began, both the families of the accused and of the victim purchased copies. They each paid $25 for their copy. They believed the document could serve as a valuable tool should an appeal be necessary. Lincoln himself purchased a copy for $27.50.

Hitt walked through Springfield now, heading to Lincoln's office. In his carpetbag, he carried, along with his clothing, the necessary tools of his trade: several new Esterbrook pens with long-lasting steel nibs, a supply of ink, and loose sheets of machine-produced paper.

The potential benefits to Lincoln's political future that could be gained with an exact transcript of the trial were many. But there was an element of risk for Lincoln even agreeing to take on this case. Up until now, Lincoln's reputation had been relatively untarnished. Of course, the consequences for Harrison should Lincoln make a major misstep were potentially life-threatening. But if Lincoln should lose the case, then the political spotlight that now focused so brightly on him might be dimmed, along with any hopes of his running for the presidency.

2

Springfield, Illinois, was a rapidly growing city. Only two decades earlier, when Lincoln had arrived there to pursue his legal career, it had been barely larger than a village. Springfield had been settled in 1819, with thick woods to the north and vast flat grassland to its south. In those early days, slightly more than a thousand residents lived in Springfield, mostly in small-frame houses and cabins. Farm animals—the pigs, especially, had an unmistakable aroma—roamed freely on black-mud streets and roads. Large chunks of wood had been laid down to help people cross streets.

But even then, as Lincoln had written in a letter to a friend, it was a place with spirit.

Springfield had always been a town that rewarded enterprise. It was a perfect place for a bright young man with passion. Lincoln eventually fit in well there. As a member of the state legislature in 1837, because of his "practical common sense [and] his thorough knowledge of human nature," wrote fellow state official Robert L. Wilson, Lincoln had been instrumental in convincing his reluctant colleagues to transfer the state capital to Springfield from the city of Vandalia.

Progress had come to Springfield slowly, but steadily. By the early 1850s, there were nearly six thousand people living there. They were connected to the world by telegraph, the railroad, and several newspapers. Impressive carriages had become common sights on the roads. Bankers had come to town, bringing with them all the necessary and desirable services and trades. Shops carried fashionable items from New York, Boston, St. Louis, and Philadelphia. It was a prosperous city now, and politicians from the various political parties often met there.

And, for those who needed to know, the Underground Railroad, which helped escaped slaves find their way to freedom, operated in Springfield, too. No one dared talk about it in public. But Lincoln's

ABRAHAM LINCOLN PRESIDENTIAL LIBRARY AND MUSEUM

The first railroad line in Springfield, Illinois, opened in 1842. This image is from 1856. By that time, trains connected Springfield to the big city of Chicago and beyond.

neighbor, a free black man named Jameson Jenkins, who lived only five doors away from Lincoln and his family, was believed to be in charge of it.

The law office of Lincoln and his younger partner, William Herndon, was in a back room on the second floor of a brick building on the northwest side of the public square, on Fifth Street. It faced the courthouse square. A small signboard on the street read "Lincoln & Herndon." It directed potential clients to a narrow stairway that led to the office.

Like most attorneys of that time, Lincoln had no

specialty. He dealt with all kinds of cases. On the same day he might write a will in the morning and defend an accused thief in the afternoon.

Hitt knew Lincoln was a man who spent a lot of time deep in thought—and as little time as possible on everyday things, like chores. So Hitt was not at all surprised when he walked into Lincoln's office and found it cluttered.

Truth be told, the office was actually well beyond cluttered. It was well beyond anything that might be fixed by a thorough cleaning. Or two. Two windows overlooking the backyard were caked so thickly with dirt and grime that they allowed very little light into the room. This could be taken as a sort of blessing. The dim light hid much of the disorder.

One young man who had done his legal training there claimed to have found plants from a forgotten bag of bean sprouts growing in a pile of dirt in a corner. A large ink blotch stained one wall. It was supposedly the result of an angry law student firing an inkstand at another's head. One visiting attorney, Henry Whitney, wrote, "No lawyer's office could have been more… untidy and uninviting than that of Lincoln and Herndon."

A long table ran lengthwise down the middle of the room, crossed at the far end by a smaller table to form a T. Both tables were covered with a faded green woolen cloth and numerous piles of papers and law books. Other piles were scattered on the floor around the office. On one stack of papers tied together with a string Lincoln had written, "When you can't find it anywhere else, look in this."

Hitt saw Lincoln stretched out full-length on two hard chairs, his eyes fixed on his notes. He was reading out loud from the pages, as he usually did.

The two men exchanged pleasantries and spoke for a while.

What daylight had managed to seep through the windows gradually disappeared. Lincoln lit two candles and began telling stories. This was the man his companions knew well, a man always ready with a story, often told at his own expense. Hitt had heard it said that no one knew the real Abraham Lincoln—he kept much of what motivated him to himself—but everyone knew his stories.

Hitt was tired from his long trip, and hungry, and he hadn't yet put his bag down in the rooming house. But there was time for all that. He was not about to give up these relaxing minutes with Abe Lincoln. And, as Hitt expected, eventually Lincoln came around to telling him about the case at hand.

3

Hitt knew the general facts because the newspapers had been writing about them. Now Lincoln added the color. Seven weeks earlier, on Saturday, July 16, Greek Crafton, a man in his early twenties, had walked into Short and Hart's drugstore in Pleasant Plains, Illinois. Pleasant Plains was about ten miles from Springfield. Greek's older brother, John Crafton, was already in the store. John was stretched out by a counter. His reason for already being there was still in dispute.

Simeon Quinn Harrison, "Peachy" as he was called, was sitting at the other counter next to Mr. Short.

Harrison was reading the newspaper. Also in his early twenties, Harrison was a frail young man, weighing no more than 125 pounds. Greek had a substantial size advantage over him.

When he came into the store, Greek was extremely angry. He took off his coat, and, along with his brother, grabbed hold of Harrison. They pulled him away from the counter. The Crafton brothers tried to drag Harrison into the back of the store. There they intended to severely thrash him, Lincoln said. Mr. Short tried to step between the boys but was pushed away by John.

Harrison struggled to break free. Greek struck him a hard blow. The brawlers fell over a pile of boxes. Harrison then pulled out a four-inch-long, white-handled hunting knife and began slashing at his attackers. Stabbing wildly, he made a deep slice into Greek's stomach. As Greek stumbled away, Harrison stabbed at John. His knife caught John on his wrist, opening a nasty cut. To keep Harrison away, John threw a balance scale, some glasses, and even a chair at him, before they could finally be separated.

Greek was seriously wounded. He had a cut from the lower rib on his left side to the groin on his right. His bowels were sticking out! Dr. J. L. Million later pushed them back into place. Greek was taken to bed, where he lingered for three days. Then he died. There never had been any real hope he would survive.

Supposedly, as Greek lay on his deathbed, he wanted to set things right. Peter Cartwright, a famous reverend—*and* Harrison's grandfather—had gone to pray with Greek. Cartwright was stunned when Greek said to him, "I brought it upon myself and I forgive Quinn, and I want it said to all my friends that I have no enmity [hate] in my heart against any man. If I die I want it declared to all that I died in peace with God and all mankind."

But even if Greek took the blame and forgave Peachy, it didn't change the fact that Greek was dead and that Peachy had delivered the fatal blow. The law would have to be involved.

After Greek died, Harrison was arrested.

Pleasant Plains was a small village of about seven hundred people. It seemed that everyone living there knew both Greek Crafton and Peachy Harrison. Each young man was from a wealthy and well-positioned farming family. A lot of people had seen both of the young men grow up, and already had an opinion about each of them. Greek could be rough sometimes, but he was a good boy at heart. Maybe he brawled from time to time, but he didn't deserve to be killed for doing what most men did.

Peachy was well liked, too. He had a friendly smile and a pleasant way about him. He wasn't a fighter like Greek, but he wasn't known for being cowardly, either.

Tempers flared in the community. Supporters of the accused and supporters of the victim each rallied behind their chosen side.

But there was even more to the story, Lincoln told Hitt. He had tried more than two thousand cases. In many of them he had known at least one of the participants, sometimes both. But he'd never had a case with as many personal connections as he did with this one.

Because Pleasant Plains was so close to Springfield, many folks in Springfield, including Lincoln, also knew Harrison and Crafton. Lincoln had known both young men for a considerable time. Peyton Harrison, the accused killer's father, was a staunch Republican and a longtime friend and supporter of Lincoln.

Lincoln and Greek had also been close. In fact, Greek had wanted to be a lawyer and had trained as a clerk at the law offices of Lincoln and Herndon.

Then, there was the Reverend Cartwright. At that time, the seventy-four-year-old reverend was perhaps even better known and more widely respected than Lincoln. For almost half a century he had traveled the frontier, bringing settlers into the Methodist religion. Many people trying to make a life in the rough fron-

THE LATE LLOYD OSTENDORF ARTWORK IS FROM THE LINCOLN COLLECTION OF THE LATE PHIL WAGNER, SPRINGFIELD, IL. IMAGE COURTESY OF WWW.ABELINCOLN.COM: ABRAHAM LINCOLN COLLECTIBLE DRAWINGS BY FAMOUS ARTIST

Lincoln had known the Harrison family for many years. In this drawing he is shown with Peachy Quinn Harrison's cousin George M. Harrison.

tier were not particularly open to the idea of religion. But it was said that Cartwright's booming voice could "make women weep and strong men tremble." Cartwright was credited with bringing many thousands of people into the fold.

People said about Cartwright, "When he thought

he was right no earthly power could persuade [him] to abandon a principle." They quickly added that Cartwright *always* thought he was right.

The problem was that Lincoln and Cartwright had been at odds for a long time. They didn't even pretend to like each other. They had run against one another in elections twice. This included Lincoln's first time running for public office. In 1832, Lincoln ran for a seat in the Illinois state legislature against Cartwright. Cartwright won.

The second time was the congressional election of 1846. It was an especially nasty campaign, during which Lincoln strongly objected to Cartwright bringing up his religion. Cartwright responded by declaring Lincoln unfit to represent good Christians. This time, Lincoln won. After it was over, neither man apologized to the other for anything that had been said.

Now the two would be on the same side in the courtroom. And this time a young man's life was at stake. This time they would have to work together, no matter their personal feelings about each other.

Lincoln knew that the whole trial might well turn on Cartwright's testimony about Greek Crafton's dying words. Surely, Lincoln told Hitt, no juror with a heart could hear those words and not be affected. But just getting those words to be heard during the trial was one of the biggest challenges facing Harrison's defense team.

Lincoln had to convince the judge to allow Cartwright to repeat Crafton's deathbed words. Under the law, these words were considered "hearsay." Hearsay is something potentially important to a case that has been said outside the courtroom by someone who—for whatever reason—cannot come to court to testify. It is considered secondhand testimony. Lawyers can ask other people who heard what was said to testify and repeat the words. But there is no way to prove that the witness is repeating the words exactly as they were said. As a result, hearsay is usually not allowed in a case.

However, one significant exception was the statement of a dying man. This exception might be traced back to the twelfth century, when it was first recognized that no man on his deathbed would tell a lie with his last breath. Through tradition it had come down through the centuries that dying declarations could be allowed but only in homicide cases, where the circumstances of the death were the subject of the declaration. Ultimately, the question of whether a dying declaration would be admissible as evidence was exclusively up to the trial judge.

Lincoln shook his head. Then he told Hitt that once Peachy and Greek had been friends. The trouble that arose between them seemed to have to do with Peachy's sister, Elizabeth Catherine. She had married Greek's brother William, and there were rumors about problems in the marriage. It looked like the seeds for the tragic event that took place on July 16 had actually been planted at least two weeks earlier.

4

On the Fourth of July, 1859, the Pleasant Plains town picnic was held on the banks of the Sangamon River. At the picnic, Peachy warned his younger brother, Peter, to stay away from the Craftons. He said they were "not fit associates." Some people maintained that Peachy slapped Greek, but only a few people supported that claim. Whether Peachy did or did not lay a hand on him, it was known that Greek was offended by the insults being made about his family. At the picnic, he challenged Peachy to a fight. Friends stepped between them before the situation burst out of control, but Greek was not satisfied. Witnesses heard him threaten to whip Peachy the next time he saw him. In reply, Peachy warned Greek that if he ever dared lay a hand on him he would defend himself—with a gun!

Rather than simmering, Lincoln went on, after the Fourth of July, the dispute began to boil. Because he was afraid of the much-larger Crafton, Harrison borrowed a knife and had it with him at all times. During the next few weeks, more insults were exchanged and the threats escalated. Until the fateful morning of the sixteenth.

After Greek died, for a time it was feared that his brother John might also die. But John pulled through.

After the fight, Harrison disappeared. He could not be found for almost a week. He had gone into hiding until his family could arrange for his legal representation. And he also was concerned for his safety. For a time Harrison's good friend, the twenty-nine-year-old city attorney Shelby Moore Cullom, hid Harrison in his home. Then Cullom hid him under the floor of the Illinois State college building!

Peyton Harrison hired a prominent former judge, Stephen Trigg Logan, to represent Peachy. Logan asked Lincoln to join him on the case. Hitt knew that few lawyers in the area were more respected than Lincoln and Logan. He believed that Harrison could not have better representation. Hitt thought, *If* my *fate was to be decided in a courtroom, these are the men I would want to defend me.*

Lincoln's current partner, Billy Herndon, himself a fine attorney, was also part of the defense. And the defense team accepted Peachy's suggestion that his friend Cullom assist them. "My duties," Cullom later remembered, "were looking up authorities and testimony and generally doing the common work of the concern."

Logan arranged for Harrison's surrender. Peachy was taken to and held in a room above the courthouse. His family paid for around-the-clock guards.

A coroner's inquest into Greek's death was held for two days, beginning on August 2. At a coroner's inquest, testimony is given to see if a crime has been committed. Was Greek's death a homicide or was it the result of a noncriminal act? As Hitt listened to Lincoln, he recalled what he had read about the inquest. As many as seventy-five witnesses had been subpoenaed, and most of them had testified.

No one disputed the fact that Peachy Quinn Harrison had stabbed Greek Crafton during a brawl in Mr. Short's store. But, was it self-defense or not?

The law defining self-defense basically stated that a man had the right to use deadly force to defend himself if he were faced with imminent and serious bodily harm or death. At the inquest, Lincoln and Logan argued that Harrison had acted in self-defense. Harrison, they maintained, had had no other choice. He had been attacked by not one, but two larger men. He had been afraid for his life.

The prosecution took the same facts and argued quite differently. They insisted that Harrison had intended to kill Crafton. During the brawl, he hadn't found and grabbed a knife. Instead, he had borrowed one prior to the encounter, and was carrying it with him. He was armed, ready, and waiting for a showdown.

Both sides argued their case with great skill. The coroner's jury ruled Greek's death a homicide. A few weeks later, the grand jury indicted Harrison for murder.

The sentence for murder was hanging.

Lincoln had not been surprised by the indictment. Feelings all around were far too raw. All the evidence would need to be presented. All the witnesses would need to be heard. If that didn't happen, then the town might never heal, he said. There would have to be a full-blown trial.

"That's the sum of it," Lincoln said finally. He walked Hitt to the Globe Tavern, where Hitt would be staying. Then Lincoln continued to walk. He savored long walks for the moments they gave him to think. At times he became so entangled in his thoughts that he completely forgot where he was going.

This evening his thoughts were focused on the coming trial. It was going to be a tricky business and would require all the skills he had developed as a lawyer. While he mourned for Greek Crafton, for all the possibilities that had been lost when he died so young, he also believed without a doubt that Peachy Harrison had acted in self-defense.

It was widely believed that Lincoln refused to defend legal positions he did not believe in. It was said he regularly turned away clients who wanted him to mold the law to fit their needs. Lincoln once avowed, "No client ever had money enough to bribe my conscience, or to stop its utterance against wrong and oppression."

Lincoln reacted strongly when people doubted the honesty of lawyers. He wrote in an 1850 essay, "There is a vague, popular belief that lawyers are necessarily dishonest... Let no young man, choosing the law for a calling, for a moment yield to this popular belief. Resolve to be honest at all events; and if, in your own judgment, you cannot be an honest lawyer, resolve to be honest without being a lawyer. Choose some other occupation..."

Honesty, above all, became Lincoln's hallmark. According to folklore, he acquired the nickname "Honest Abe" while working as a store clerk in New Salem, Illinois. He had walked several miles to return a few pennies due a customer.

In this case, Lincoln's firm belief that Peachy had acted in self-defense was based in no small part on the visit he and Logan had paid the young man when he was being held in the room above the courthouse. The room's sloping roof had made it impossible for Lincoln to stand tall wearing his hat. The room had a single bed, a chair, and a rather large window. The clouds were covering the sun and a gray, dull light came through the window, which seemed fitting for the somber mood.

Peachy stood to greet Lincoln and Logan. He brushed his hands on his buckskin trousers before politely shaking Lincoln's hand.

"Well, this is a sorry matter," Lincoln said.

Harrison stared at the floor, nodding.

"I've known your family since afore you were born," Lincoln continued. "Practically before your father was born."

"Grandpap told me that. He said you keep hard opinions, but that you and Mr. Logan were the best law people around here."

Lincoln chuckled. "Well, we've had our differences

for sure, your grandfather and me. So where's that name come from, Peachy?"

The young man smiled for the first time. "Always had it, since I was a boy. It's just an old family name, sir. There's been lots of Peachys among the Harrisons, both men and women. I even got an aunt called Peachy."

"You know I knew Greek Crafton," Lincoln said. "He studied the law in my office."

"I think he told me. We were friends sometimes." Peachy paused. He sighed deeply, then added, "Till all this."

"Why don't you tell us what happened. Just let it out."

And so Peachy did.

"Didn't mean for it to happen," he said. He raised his right hand. "Swear to God. Nobody did. But I guess it just couldn't be helped."

It had indeed started at the Fourth of July picnic. It was on account of family matters, the trouble in the marriage of William Crafton and Eliza Harrison. Peachy had said some nasty things. Greek had responded. Everything quickly escalated. Threats were made, and neither young man knew how to back away with his pride intact.

Tears welled in Harrison's eyes as he continued. "One on one I wasn't much afraid of him," he said.

"Maybe I couldn't lick him straight up, but I would do okay. But the two of them, that wasn't right." He had borrowed the knife. No, he hadn't meant to use it. It was just for protection, to keep them away.

On July 16 he was already in the store when John Crafton walked in. He saw him, but it wasn't John who had been making threats, so he wasn't concerned. When Greek came in, though, he knew there was going to be trouble.

Greek threw his arms around him, and Peachy took hold of the counter railing. He figured that as long as he held on there wasn't much Greek could do to him. After that, well, things just started happening fast. He didn't even remember going for the knife, he said.

Logan asked, "You're pretty good with a knife, right?"

Harrison considered that, perhaps sensing the danger in the question and not sure how to answer it. "I grew up with them, if that's what you mean. We all did. You know, when I was out on the farm. But I never ever cut nobody ever. I sure didn't mean to cut Greek like that, to hurt him like that. I just wanted to keep him away from me.

"He said he was gonna stomp my face," Harrison added.

"Who told you that?" Logan asked.

Peachy hesitated, scrunching his face as he struggled for an answer. "You know, everybody. It was around. Everybody was talking."

Logan led Harrison through the events, at one point asking him to stand up and show them the stabbing exactly as it had happened.

Lincoln softly asked Peachy, "Are you scared?"

Peachy nodded, his eyes watering once again. "Yes, sir, I am. Really scared."

"Good, that's a truthful answer. You're right to be. This is a dangerous matter. There's no need for us to hide from that. But if we all do our job, this is going to turn out right for us."

Lincoln acknowledged and respected Peachy for being honest with him. And Lincoln carried his strong respect for and commitment to the truth with him into every courtroom for every trial. Judges, fellow lawyers, and jurors came to know the value of his word.

There is little doubt that Lincoln's reputation served his clients well. This was especially important, because at that time, under the law in Illinois, a defendant could not take the stand on his own behalf!

Simeon "Peachy" Quinn Harrison would not be allowed to say one word during his own trial.

5

There isn't any specific time or event historians can point to and say, "Right there—that's when Abraham Lincoln decided to become a lawyer." He tried his hand at several other professions first. He was a store clerk, a deckhand and a captain on riverboats, a postmaster, a shopkeeper, a farm laborer, and a surveyor. The law finally caught his fancy and he committed himself to it. The law was considered an honorable trade. You trained for it, and didn't necessarily need formal schooling.

When asked, years after he had begun practicing for advice on how to enter the profession, Lincoln wrote,

"If you are resolutely determined to make a lawyer of yourself, the thing is more than half already done. It is but a small matter whether you read with anybody or not. I did not read with anyone. Get the books and study them till you understand them in their principal features... Work, work, work is the main thing."

The only requirement for a license to practice law was a certificate granted by a court. It certified that the applicant was a man of good moral character. The Circuit Court of Sangamon County certified Abraham Lincoln as "a person of good moral character" on March 1, 1837. Lincoln raised his right hand and took an oath to support the Constitution of the United States, and the state of Illinois. Several months later, his name was published in the annual listing of attorneys, and he was allowed to practice.

Armed with this credential, Lincoln rode into Springfield on a borrowed horse. He set down his saddlebags in the bedroom above Joshua Speed's store and set to practicing general law with his first law partner, John Todd Stuart. They pretty much did whatever legal work was needed.

Lincoln learned by doing. He defended debtors and pressed debt collections. He created and dissolved partnerships, incorporated companies, and declared bankruptcies. He wrote wills and defended petty thieves and men charged with brawling. He won some and lost some, and he slowly built a practice. Lincoln and men like him brought the structure and accountability provided by the law to what was then the west.

Lincoln and Stuart's second-floor office was conveniently located directly over the county courthouse. In fact, there was a trapdoor in the office. One evening, a friend of Lincoln's, E. D. Baker, was making a passionate political speech. Lincoln watched from above. He lay on the floor of his office and peered through the trapdoor.

Baker's speech angered the crowd. Several men moved forward, seemingly ready to attack him. But they stopped as two long legs suddenly dangled from the ceiling. They were followed by all of Lincoln's six-foot-four-inch frame coming through the trapdoor. Lincoln dropped into the courtroom and stood between the men and Baker. He warned, "Mr. Baker has a right to speak…and no man shall take him from this platform if I can prevent it."

No one doubted either what he had said or his ability to do it.

When Lincoln's partnership with Stuart ended in 1841, he joined forces with Stephen Trigg Logan. Logan was a former circuit court judge and perhaps the most respected lawyer in Illinois. In fact, it was

Judge Logan who had signed the court register officially adding Lincoln to the list of lawyers. He had sat in judgment on several of Lincoln's early cases. And the two men had previously worked together on the first of Lincoln's murder trials.

The case was the 1838 shooting of Dr. Jacob M. Earley by Henry Truett. There seemed to be little question about the facts. Earley had been sitting in the parlor of Spottswood's Rural Hotel when Truett entered. To avenge a perceived insult, he pulled his pistol and shot Earley. Earley lingered for three days. Before he died, he named Truett as his killer.

The defense team included Stuart, Lincoln, and Logan. And the acting prosecutor was none other than the same Stephen Douglas who Lincoln would later debate and run against for Illinois senator.

Much like the Harrison case decades later, this crime divided Springfield. There were several suggestions of a motive, but political differences clearly were at the core.

As the trial went on, evidence against Truett piled up. The prosecution introduced a motive, and produced evidence that Truett had planned the crime. They convinced the judge to admit Earley's dying declaration. The outcome seemed certain—until summations began.

Lawyers were showmen, even back then. The courtroom was their stage. The favored style of the day was that of the greatest stage actors of the time. Lawyers thundered and raged, they whispered and wept, they waved their arms and pounded the table. They performed, and the verdict they wanted was their reward.

But Lincoln brought a different style into the courtroom. He didn't do much in the way of drama. Even though he towered above most jurors, it never seemed like he was looking down on them. When he approached the jury box and leaned over close, he was just talking to some friends.

Even in his early years of practice, Lincoln's stirring use of common language allowed him to forge a remarkable connection with his audience.

In the Truett case, Lincoln showed jurors a different way to look at the facts. He suggested to them the possibility of following an alternative path. Lincoln had known the victim, and he undoubtedly told the jury that this was a sorry affair. There was no doubt about that. But, Lincoln insisted, his client had acted in self-defense. The victim had been holding a chair, Lincoln argued. The chair was potentially a lethal weapon.

After five days of mostly negative testimony against Truett, they needed only three hours to reach a verdict.

Not guilty.

Lincoln was given substantial credit for the outcome, which greatly improved his professional prospects. His practice continued to grow steadily.

When his association with Logan ended after three years, Lincoln formed a partnership with Herndon, whose family he had known for a decade. Their partnership would continue in some way until Lincoln was assassinated in 1865.

6

It was the first day of the Peachy Quinn Harrison murder trial. Hitt made his way the three blocks from the Globe Tavern across the public square to the Sangamon County Courthouse on Sixth and Washington. A large crowd had already gathered outside. Everyone expected that the trial was going to be a humdinger, and no one wanted to miss a word of it. For those who had nothing at stake, a trial was considered entertainment. On "court day" the galleries in the courtroom were often packed with spectators.

Hitt walked quickly up the courthouse steps. Several men recognized him. "That's Lincoln's steno man," he

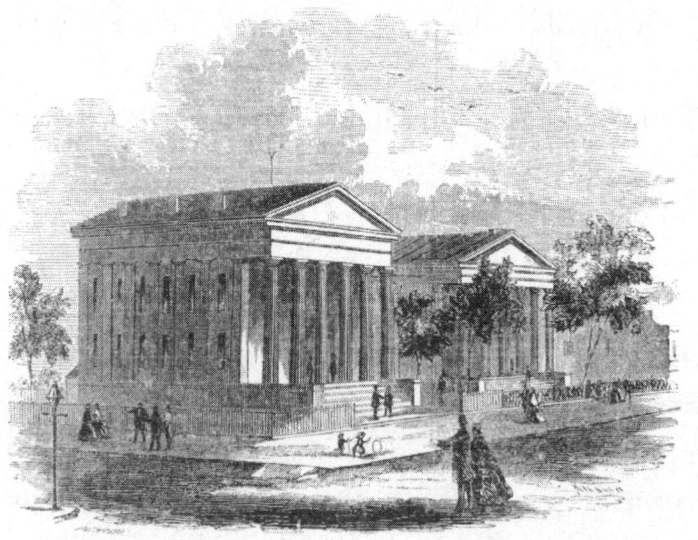

ABRAHAM LINCOLN PRESIDENTIAL LIBRARY AND MUSEUM

The courthouse where Lincoln's last murder trial took place. Over the years Lincoln tried several hundred cases in this building.

heard someone say. Hitt blushed slightly, but he kept looking forward and didn't stop.

Hitt knew there would not be much work for him today. The first day of any trial, and perhaps even the second, would be about motions and jury selection. Transcripts had not been requested for these stages.

During this time, the presiding judge would set the tone of the trial. Each judge had his own opinion as to how a trial should be conducted. Some of them "locked the doors." This meant they kept strictly to the letter of the law. Other judges "let chickens in to play"—they allowed almost anything within reason to help the jury reach a fair verdict.

The judge in this case, Judge Edward Y. Rice, had earned a reputation as strict but fair. Although Lincoln would never say so out loud, Hitt was pretty sure he was not pleased to have Judge Rice presiding in the case. Judge Rice was not one of those judges who appreciated good courtroom wit or just let lawyers have their say. He kept a tight rein on the proceedings. Lincoln preferred a looser courtroom. He wanted to be able to make a friendly comment now and then that could help him build a relationship with jurors.

Hitt climbed the steps to the second-floor courtroom. The large wooden double doors had been tied open. Hitt entered and glanced around the courtroom. His previous steno work had all been in Chicago courtrooms. They were fancier than this one, but they were all laid out the same. He had read somewhere that the layout was based on the British justice system. The judge sat at the head of the courtroom on a raised platform called a bench. The witness stand was next to the bench. The lawyers, the accused, and most of the court officials sat or stood in front of the judge's bench. They were separated from the spectator gallery by a low rail called the bar.

Lincoln was already in the courtroom when Hitt entered. He was standing with a group of people over

LIBRARY OF CONGRESS, PRINTS & PHOTOGRAPHS DIVISION, HABS, HABS ILL,9-BEATO,3-

Abraham Lincoln had been a lawyer on an earlier case in this courtroom in the Cass County Courthouse in Beardstown, Illinois. The courtroom for his last trial probably looked very similar.

by the jury box. They were chatting before the proceedings began.

Lincoln wore a black frock coat, dark trousers slightly too short for his long bony legs, and dirty black shoes. His tie was slung to one side and his hair was uncombed.

The group by the jury box included other members of the defense team. Members of the prosecution were also present, including John M. Palmer. Palmer and Lincoln often found themselves as legal adversaries. But there was still a strong bond between them.

Both men had been raised in Kentucky. Each had come to Springfield to practice law and politics. Palmer had served a term in the state legislature as a Democrat, but later joined the new Republican Party.

There were several other men Hitt did not recognize. He assumed that one of them was J. B. White, Illinois's fairly new state attorney and one of the lawyers for the prosecution in this case. Lincoln and White had also faced each other in a courtroom before.

Just two years earlier, White was the prosecutor for a case in which Lincoln had defended someone accused of firing a shotgun into a crowd and killing a well-liked man. There was a great deal of public outrage against his client. Lincoln asked for and was granted additional time to gather reluctant witnesses. He also requested that the trial be moved because of all the public attention. This request was also granted. It, too, resulted in a trial delay.

Lincoln then went on to declare that the case should be dismissed. He argued that the accused had been denied his constitutional right to a speedy trial! By the time White figured out what Lincoln was up to, it was too late to do anything about it. All charges against the accused were dropped.

With the Harrison case, White, no doubt, was going

to be at the top of his game where Lincoln was concerned.

John McClernand and Norman M. Broadwell rounded out the prosecution team.

Hitt took his seat in front of the judge's bench. Spectators filled all the seats and standing room in the back and on the sides of the courtroom. There were few women among the spectators. Men who had seats stood and offered them to the women. In addition, Hitt saw two black men sitting freely in the courtroom. He couldn't remember ever seeing a black face among the spectators in a Chicago courtroom.

The room was nearly overfilled by the time Judge Rice entered the courtroom.

Just moments before the judge gaveled the proceedings to order, Harrison was brought into the courtroom. His wrists were handcuffed. The marshal removed the handcuffs, and Harrison took his seat at the desk between Lincoln and Logan. To Hitt, Harrison looked as frail as a leaf. Hitt suspected that Harrison's appearance had been carefully planned. Lincoln wanted Harrison to look too small, too weak to have stood his ground against an angry, hulking foe or foes. Logan whispered something to Harrison. Peachy smiled faintly. Then he turned around to greet several people sitting in the front row. One of them, Hitt was certain, was the Reverend Cartwright, Peachy's grandfather.

Lincoln reached for his tall hat, which sat on the table. He often carried his legal papers in that hat. Sure enough, he withdrew several sheets of paper from the hat. He began to busily arrange the papers in front of him.

At half past the hour of nine the court crier, T. S. Kidd, shouted, "Hear ye! Hear ye! Hear ye! Court is now in session. Judge Edward Rice presiding. God save the United States and this honorable court."

7

Judge Rice greeted the participants. Then he cautioned the spectators that he would tolerate no outbursts. Next he called for jury selection to begin immediately.

At the time, the law in Illinois specified that jurors had to be white, male, property-owning American citizens between the ages of twenty-one and sixty. The daily pay for a juror was a then respectable $1.50.

The jury panel for this trial had been summoned from the city and nearby farms. It was considered an unfair burden to make people who lived way out in the county fulfill their jury duty.

In general, it seemed that people were not always eager to serve on a jury. In fact, there were times when the court had to send marshals into the streets to bring back any bystanders they could find. That was not true in this case. The difficulty here would be finding twelve impartial jurors, since so many people knew either or both Harrison and Crafton.

A good lawyer knew to take great care in selecting a jury. In an earlier murder case, Lincoln had spent three days picking the jury. He then took only one day to make his case in front of them. He got the acquittal he wanted.

It is said that every great defense lawyer has a feel for those jurors most likely to be sympathetic to his case. It's an intuition developed over a long period of time and experience. Lincoln was no different. He had his own way of determining who might be in tune with him.

Sometimes he based this just on a potential juror's physical appearance. Lincoln did not want blond, blue-eyed men on his jury. He believed that type of man to be a bit nervous and too easily led by the prosecution in violent cases. Over time he had formed a prejudice against men with high foreheads. He found that too often these men formed an early opinion. He found it hard to get them to change their minds. Lincoln actually liked having overweight men on his jury. It was generally believed that men of great size had gotten ahead by using their wits. That was the kind of man who might appreciate the delicacy of Lincoln's arguments and approach to a case.

Finally, whenever possible, Lincoln wanted young men on his juries rather than older men. His clients were often of a similar young age, and Lincoln felt young jurors might relate better to them. And older men, he found—men like himself—were often too set in their ways to be moved.

While most often the jury selection process was repetitive and dull, this time Hitt actually was looking forward to it. He was eager to watch Lincoln begin building his relationship with the jurors.

The lawyers took turns asking questions of potential jurors to determine if a candidate could judge the case fairly. If one side decided they wanted to seat a juror, the other side could agree, or they could challenge the choice. Each side had several challenges they could make. Unless one side ran out of challenges, both sides had to approve the selection of each juror. The judge had the right to reject any juror he so chose. The questions included:

"Do you know the defendant or his family?"

"Did you know the decedent [or, as the prosecution pointedly described Greek Crafton, 'the victim'] or his family?"

"What is it you do to earn a living?"

The first juror selected was Charles D. Nukolls. He was one of the oldest, best-known, and more respected citizens of the city. Mr. Nukolls had settled in the area decades earlier and worked in the leather business. More recently Nukolls had graduated from McDowell College in St. Louis with a degree in medicine. His Republican politics were well-known, which obviously pleased Lincoln. There simply was no way either side could challenge his ability to judge fairly in this case.

The questions continued:

"Do you consider yourself a political man?"

"You think the leanings of any of these people [indicating the lawyers] will influence your ability to be fair-minded?"

"Have you read about this case in the newspapers?"

The second man seated was Josephus Gatton. Like Lincoln, he had come to Illinois from Kentucky. He was a successful farmer who then bought more land. He had large houses built on the land. He, too, was one of the wealthier men in the city. And, as with Nukolls, he was a perfectly appropriate choice.

By the end of the morning two more men had been

selected. One of them, Moses Pilcher, was considered to be the best carpenter in the city. He had also been a political ally of Lincoln for decades.

The fourth juror was Isaac Payton. Payton was a widower struggling to farm a small spread with his two young boys. He was also working as a shipping clerk for the new Wabash railroad line. Neither side wanted to deprive him of the juror's pay. It was sure to help him pay down some debts.

That afternoon, as the heat rose, the jury box continued to be filled. Zenas Bramwell fit Lincoln's desire for an overweight man. Bob Cass became juror number six. He had one of the larger farms in the county, and was known to be a stern but honest man. Cass was approved without challenge. Ben Brown, a farmer with a prized bull named George II, took his place in the jury box. He sat next to George Robinson, another farmer. William Patterson, the next juror selected, was a Scottish immigrant who had been in America for a decade. He worked with his cousin on a farm and was now a citizen.

Lincoln shared the questioning for the defense team with Logan and Cullom. Hitt noticed that even when Lincoln was just sitting and listening, he was still completely involved. It was clear Lincoln was a casual man, even in court. On occasion he stretched backward and his very large black shoes would suddenly appear from beneath his wooden desk.

At different times, everyone in the courtroom had to fight to stifle a yawn. Hitt himself yawned more than once. But if Lincoln yawned, too, the steno man didn't see him do it. Sometimes Lincoln stared straight ahead. Sometimes his hands were clasped behind his neck and his eyes seemed riveted on a point on the ceiling. Sometimes he was leaning forward on his right elbow, his thumb beneath his chin and his index finger curving along his cheekbone. But it was clear that even in this dullest part of the trial, he was paying close attention.

The afternoon droned on. Farmer William Hinchey drew hearty laughs when, asked if he knew the details of the case, he responded firmly, "I don't know nuthin' about nuthin'!" He looked proudly at the gallery and grinned a wide, mostly toothless grin. When both sides agreed to place him on the jury, the gallery cheered.

Farmer Jefferson Pierce was the eleventh man to be selected.

The final selection was twenty-two-year-old farmer M. H. Pickrell. He was the youngest member of the jury. He was also the 101st man to be questioned that day!

It was now early evening. Judge Rice made a few

remarks warning the jury not to discuss the case with anyone. He was about to dismiss court for the day when Bob Cass raised his hand. He was feeling poorly, he said. He asked to be excused. His word was good enough for his request to be granted without any objection.

At the time, there was no law requiring that a jury have twelve men. But both sides agreed that a twelve-man jury was preferable. So everybody had to sit a little longer.

Most of the remaining candidates had scattered. Lincoln and Palmer agreed to seat James A. Brundage. Brundage was a bystander who had been watching the proceedings, and who already knew both Lincoln and Palmer.

By this time everyone was ready to head home. Judge Rice reminded everyone to be back in the courtroom at exactly nine o'clock in the morning, or at least as close as they could make it. Then he gaveled the day closed.

8

The next morning, a steady stream of people made their way to the courthouse. After an early rainstorm, the air was filled with humidity.

Hitt was in his seat, his pens a-ready, when, close to 9:00 a.m., Judge Rice pronounced the court in session. The session began with a discussion about whether or not witnesses should be allowed to stay in the courtroom when other witnesses were testifying. In a Motion for Sequestration, witnesses are prevented from hearing anyone else's testimony because it might influence their own.

It was agreed by both sides that one man, the Reverend Cartwright, would be permitted to remain before and after he testified. The other witnesses would only be allowed in the courtroom for their own testimony.

The prosecution called its first witness, Dr. John L. Million. The thirty-two-year-old doctor was a small, bearded man with spectacles. Palmer stood behind his desk and began the questioning.

The trial had begun.

After asking Dr. Million a few basic questions about himself and Crafton and Harrison, Palmer got to the heart of the matter.

"Is it true...is it...that Greek Crafton is dead?"

The doctor grimaced, then nodded.

"What do you know of the cause of his death?"

This was a question Dr. Million had been well prepped for by the prosecution to answer. If Million described the crime in bloody detail, the prosecution hoped the fury and brutality of the attack would disgust the jury. "He died from a wound inflicted in his side, I believe between the eleventh and twelfth ribs on the left side." Dr. Million poked that place on his own body with his left hand.

"That wound penetrated into the cavity of the abdomen," the doctor said. "We could not ascertain positively what organs were injured, but we supposed from the course the knife took that the spleen and the stomach were penetrated."

"When were you called to see him?"

"Well, sir," Million said, "I saw him, I suppose, a minute or two after this accident.

"He was out in front of the drugstore where the difficulty took place. This drugstore was in Pleasant Plains and belonged at the time, I believe, to Short and Hart. When I first saw him, he was in rather a staggering condition, when I caught him. He called to me. I ran up to him and he reclined on me in a rather failing position. I don't recollect which side. He was then taken to my house by myself and one or two other gentlemen in Pleasant Plains. I suppose it is something like a hundred yards from the drugstore, probably not quite so far."

Palmer led Million through the testimony. "Was an examination made of his condition?"

Million squared his shoulders. "His intestines," he said, sighing at the memory. "A portion of them were protruding, and I returned them to their place and dressed the wound, taking two or three stitches and applied some plaster over it."

Several people in the gallery gasped at Million's report, but Hitt did not show any response as he wrote it all down.

After a pause, Palmer continued, "Did you make an examination of his person at that time?"

"No further than the wound, and I think the seventh and eighth rib. It looked like a knife had struck against a rib a very slight wound. I should suppose these wounds had been made by a sharp pointed knife."

The description of the weapon as a "sharp pointed knife" was surely meant to have an impact on the jurors. The intended meaning was that a sharp and pointed weapon was meant for attacking, not for protection. But Lincoln did not object.

Palmer next asked about the direction of the cut. "It was being between two ribs, it was difficult to say, only from symptoms which way the course was," said Million. "We imagined that the knife took a horizontal direction. It would be horizontal if he was standing erect..."

Hitt chanced a quick glance at the jury. Most of them were sitting expressionless but focused.

Dr. Million continued, "About an hour and a half after the injury he vomited a large quantity of blood and that could not, I suppose, have got into the stomach without the stomach had been cut. It might have cut the duodenum."

Du-o-de-num was a term Hitt did not know. It was obviously a part of the body. He spelled it phonetically, hoping he would be able to find it in the edition of Noah Webster's dictionary he carried with him for just such a purpose.

"When was that?" Palmer asked.

"Saturday morning the sixteenth of July of the present year, 1859. In Sangamon County."

"You stated it was soon after the blow. Why did you come to that conclusion?"

"I saw Greek Crafton that morning. I think…on the street. From the app…" Someone in the gallery began coughing and Hitt lost the remainder of that word. As he had been taught, the professional does not make assumptions. In a courtroom every word is important. He was certain the word was *appearance* but did not mark it down. "…of the wound was inflicted between seven and eight o'clock, not noticing the time particularly, and he died, sir, about eight o'clock Monday night. I think the death was caused by the wound."

"Do you know anything about the circumstances of the infliction of the wound?"

"I do not of my own knowledge."

"Are you a practicing physician?"

"Yes, sir."

Palmer, having established that Crafton had been knifed to death, dismissed the witness. Judge Rice cautioned Dr. Million to speak with no one about his testimony.

Neither Lincoln nor Logan objected a single time during the doctor's testimony. It had been a violent scene. It was all too easy for jurors to imagine the doctor stuffing Crafton's intestines back into his body, and the victim vomiting blood. There was no way to disguise that. There was no point in disputing it. In addition, it was the accepted custom of the day to let each side have its say, with few objections. And, when the time came, what the doctor had said would not impact Lincoln's defense.

9

Palmer called Silas Livergood to the stand. Livergood had been an eyewitness to the crime. A friend of Greek and John Crafton, Livergood had gone to the store that morning with Greek.

After he was sworn in, Palmer asked Livergood to tell his account of what had happened between Crafton and Harrison.

"Well, when I first saw them at the drugstore, they were together. Greek Crafton had hold of Harrison around the arm. He was back of Harrison. Harrison had hold of the counter." Asked what was said during the fight, Livergood responded, "I didn't hear Mr.

Crafton say anything. Mr. Harrison allowed that he didn't want to fight or wouldn't fight him, I can't tell exactly."

Crafton did not reply, Livergood continued. He then described their positions. "Well, Crafton had hold of him at the time they were at the counter and I think Mr. Short had hold of him when Harrison made that remark."

With a piece of white chalk Palmer drew a rough diagram of the store on the floor. He then handed Livergood a long wooden cane and asked him to point out to the jury where this had taken place. Several jurors in the second row stood to see better. Logan stood, too. Lincoln stayed seated, but leaned forward.

"This is the north end and this is the south," Livergood said as he poked the floor. "Here is the entrance on the north side and now there is where they were standing. There was a counter on the east side of that."

For clarity, again as he had been taught, Hitt added in parentheses that the counter was "running north and south."

Livergood pointed to the spot near the counter where Harrison and Crafton were fighting. "Harrison was holding onto the counter. Crafton had him around the arms."

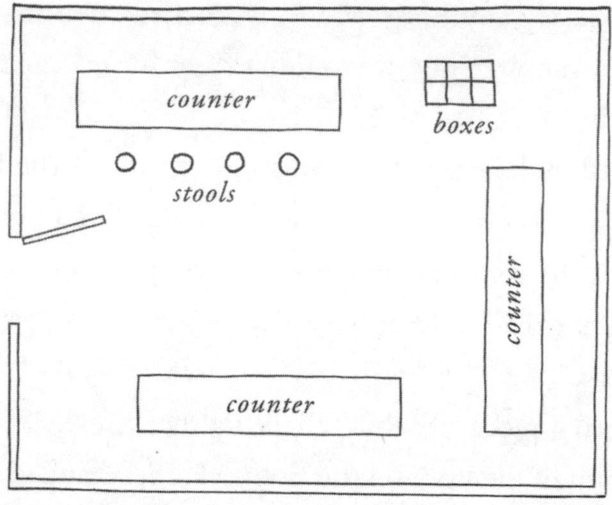

Like the diagram Palmer drew on the floor of the courtroom, this one shows the layout of Short and Hart's drugstore.

"What was Short doing?" Palmer asked, building his crime scene.

"He was not doing much of anything. He had hold of them, trying to part them. Both of them, I think."

"Did you see the hands of either party?"

"I saw the hands of Harrison. I am not certain but of Crafton. Directly after that John Crafton interfered and took hold of Short."

Using the cane, Livergood indicated that John Crafton "was about this part of the store." Once again, Hitt further described the location "back" to convey the complete response. "As soon as Mr. Short took hold he interfered and he made the remark that 'Greek could' or 'should whip him' or something to that effect. Then they retreated to the back part of the store. Here was another counter. They all went together to the back part of the store."

"Where were you standing?"

"About there, in the front part of the store. Harrison was nearest me as they were retreating... They retreated in front of this back counter," Livergood continued, pointing. "There were some boxes standing there and they retreated to the boxes and there Crafton got into a leaning position and the cutting was done there."

This testimony clearly was key. Lincoln propped his elbows on the table, and his palms formed a church in front of him as he listened intently.

"I don't know what placed them there," Livergood continued. "I saw Harrison at the time. He was in the same position in which he was when he started, with his back to them. He had not changed his position. Harrison did the cutting. I saw it. Crafton was in a leaning position. He was leaning over the boxes half down." Livergood leaned over to demonstrate.

Hitt was not a lawyer, but he realized the danger of this testimony to Harrison. By Livergood's account, Peachy was in no obvious danger. He was being pushed around, but neither his life nor even his safety was threatened. And yet, he had responded with deadly force.

With this piece of testimony Palmer had what he was looking for. But he continued, his pace a little quicker. "How were the blows struck?"

"Harrison was standing on the east of Crafton and he struck him right in the side. Crafton was inclined in this way." He turned to his side and glanced at the jury to ensure they understood. "Harrison stood right in front. I saw two blows struck with a knife."

Palmer paused to allow that information to sink in. Two blows. Not one. Not an accident. Two blows. And then he asked, "What was Crafton doing when he was struck?"

It was an important question. Livergood answered in a voice tinged with anger and accusation, "He was not doing anything. He was in that inclined position. I saw the knife. It was a white-handled knife."

"Had anybody hold of Harrison when he struck the blow?" Palmer asked next.

"Yes, sir. Greek Crafton had hold of him by his left arm."

"Assuming that I was Harrison, how did he have hold of him?"

Livergood left the witness stand. Palmer turned

around to directly face the jury. Livergood took a position behind him and swept his left arm around his body, pinning Palmer's left arm. "Crafton had hold of him something like that, with his arm around his arm."

Still looking directly at the jury, Palmer asked, "With which hand did he strike?"

"With his right hand. It was loose at the time."

"How long had that hand been loose?"

"Just then."

"Had you observed it before that?"

"Yes."

"Was anything in it?"

"No, sir. There was nothing in that hand."

"In what position was Crafton when the knife was drawn?"

"The same position he was when he was cut."

All this while Livergood retained his hold on Palmer. The visual evidence was strong. Harrison was not in danger for his life. Crafton was holding him. He was not choking him or stomping him or punching him. He was just restraining him. It was what happened dozens of times a day when children fought.

"How long did they remain there?" Palmer asked.

"They did not remain there."

Palmer removed Livergood's arm from around his body and the two men separated. Livergood took the witness chair again and continued, "I could hardly tell how they were separated. I know I went toward them and helped separate them."

"What happened after the blows were struck?"

"I don't know as Mr. Short did anything. If he did I didn't see him do anything. Greek Crafton got out of the house [store] and directly after Greek was cut, John was cut. John was making toward Quinn when he was cut."

"Where was John when Greek was cut?"

"John was behind Quinn like. He was in a leaning position too. Mr. Short had hold of Greek and Quinn. He let them go immediately after the cutting was done. After Short let him go, Greek got out of the house and John commenced throwing a pair of scales at him [Harrison], and a stool. They were all loosened up when John was cut. When John received the blow he stood to the south of Harrison and Greek to the west of him... I think that was the position they were in at the time."

"You spoke of John throwing something. Was that before or after he was cut with the knife?"

Livergood answered firmly, "After he was cut with the knife."

Palmer leaned back in his seat and allowed a few

seconds to pass before nodding to Judge Rice. He had no more questions.

The judge pointed to the defense table. Logan stood to begin the cross-examination.

10

Logan stood directly in front of the witness. He asked, "Was there not a little circumstance you omitted? You say as they went back Greek had hold of Quinn with both hands?" Livergood acknowledged that was true.

Logan continued, "You said when he drew his knife Greek had but one [hand] around him?" That, too, was true. "How long was it before Quinn struck did he take his hand away?"

"Immediately."

"What did Greek do when he took his right arm from around Quinn?"

"Greek struck him in the face." Hitt kept his head down, so no one would see his smile. So that's what Logan was after.

"Immediately after Greek struck him in the face he drew the knife."

Logan pressed on. "Did Greek give him a pretty severe blow before he drew the knife?" That was it. That was key to it. Several jurors in the first row leaned forward.

"I don't know," Livergood answered. He was being honest. Or he had been too well prepped by Palmer's team to answer otherwise. "I can't speak for that."

"Did you see the mark?" Logan asked, implying that Greek had struck such a strong blow as to leave a mark.

"No, sir."

"It was not until Greek keeping hold with his left and letting go with his right hand struck him in the face that he drew his knife?"

"No, sir, but immediately after that Quinn drew his knife."

Logan was showing that Harrison had indeed been in real danger. He was carefully countering the damage that Palmer had done to the defense with Livergood's testimony.

Logan looked at the jury as he asked this next question, to make sure they understood its importance.

"The first thing you heard when you went in was by Quinn, 'I don't want to fight you and I won't fight you?'"

Palmer sat still as Livergood agreed that was correct. "Yes. Greek still held onto him and he held onto the counter."

Logan was drawing a strong picture of Harrison desperately trying to protect himself. He said clearly he did not want this fight. He held onto the counter to try to prevent it.

"What broke him loose?" asked Logan.

"Mr. Short and John Crafton interfering. That pulled Short back. Short, I suppose, was trying to separate them and John interfered."

"To prevent their being separated?"

Livergood shook his head. "I don't know about that."

Logan continued, "John made the remark that, 'Greek could whip him and should whip him'?"

"Yes, sir. I don't say that that is exactly the words. When they retreated back the balance took Quinn back I suppose. He was dragged back from the counter."

This was the point Logan was trying to emphasize: Harrison did not want this fight. "Was he not dragged back with such force as to break his hold on the counter?"

Livergood shrugged as he answered, his reluctance visible.

"Yes, I suppose so. I think he was holding onto the bar of the counter."

Lincoln stood and glanced down as if he was reading from nonexistent notes. Then he asked, "How long had Greek Crafton been in before you went in and saw him with his arms around Quinn?"

"Only a little while. I started from Turley's store with him."

"What was said when you started about what you were going for?"

Livergood answered strongly, "Nothing was said at the time."

Lincoln persisted, "Did you go in concert with Greek Crafton?"

"No, sir! He asked me to go along with him. He did not tell me what for."

"Objection, your honor!" Palmer stood, waving his hands.

"This is not proper cross-examination."

It was here that Hitt saw a sure glimpse of the defense case. Lincoln intended to show that when Greek Crafton found out Harrison was at Short's store, he set out to attack him. But he wasn't going alone. There were three of them: Greek, John, and Livergood.

Lincoln told Judge Rice that he was going to make the case that his client had good reason to be afraid for his safety. He was firm in that, he said. And he could either show it now or later.

Palmer reminded the judge that his witness had been clear that was not at all the situation.

Judge Rice ruled that this was not the proper time, or witness, for Lincoln to prove that. "Bring it in on your own witnesses," he told him.

Having had his say, and confident that the point had been made to the jury, Lincoln sat down.

Logan resumed questioning Livergood, who spent the remainder of the morning on the witness stand. There were many more questions about the precise positioning of the participants and the timing of the events.

When the morning session ended, Palmer was quite satisfied. The prosecution had demonstrated to the jury the fury of the attack and had shown them how it happened. Nothing in the demonstrations, either his own or those staged by the defense, positioned Harrison in any life-threatening way. In fact, it seemed like Mr. Short was trying to break up the fight when the stabbing took place.

Lincoln and Logan were also satisfied. They had planted the seeds for their case. They had filled the room with the Crafton brothers and Livergood, suggesting they were all out to beat Harrison. Harrison surely had had no choice but to defend himself. The defense had limited the damage from this eyewitness's testimony.

Livergood finally stepped down off the witness stand. Hitt watched him walk past the lawyers' table to the gallery. As Livergood passed Harrison he glanced at him and acknowledged him with a slight nod. When he got to the back of the courtroom, Livergood was surrounded by a group of young men who pounded his back and assured him he had done right by Greek.

Lincoln and Logan sat at their table, both of them facing Harrison. Hitt guessed they were reassuring him. Hitt wondered what must be running through Harrison's mind. How was he dealing with feeling the breath of death at such a young age—and all because of an unnecessary act?

11

Judge Rice called for a brief break. When the trial resumed, the prosecution called John Crafton, Greek's brother, who had been at the center of it all.

John's right arm was in a bright red handkerchief sling. When he placed his right hand on a bible to take the oath, Hitt noticed that John's right wrist was also wrapped in a bandage.

Palmer led Crafton through the basics. Crafton said that he lived at home with his parents, Wiley and Agnes Crafton, about a mile north of Pleasant Plains in Sangamon County. Yes, he knew Peachy Quinn

Harrison. He last saw his brother after breakfast on the sixteenth of July. John had gone into Pleasant Plains. Greek had started to Berlinsville, for reasons he had not mentioned. John had next seen him at Mr. Turley's store, then soon afterward again at the drugstore.

Palmer asked Crafton to "Begin at that point at which you went to the drugstore and tell what you went there for, when your brother came, and what took place." In many courtrooms of that time, questions like this that might have long and rambling answers were permitted. It was not like today, where many questions require either a simple yes or no answer or an answer of few words.

Giving a witness the freedom to have his or her say was an approach respected by both sides. The witness was rarely interrupted. There were moments when this sort of testimony might unintentionally wind up helping the opposition: a witness might become too comfortable and chatty and add unnecessary details that could weaken his own side's case.

Crafton's response was long and rich with those sorts of details. While he was talking, he also got up and pointed at various places on the diagram of the drugstore that had been drawn on the courtroom floor.

"I went there as my business was for money," he began. "I called upon Mr. Short to know if any money had been left for me. He said not with him. He told me probably it was left with Mr. Hart, his partner. I asked where Mr. Hart was. He said in town somewhere. I said no more to him. Yes, I says, I'll wait for him here and I passed to the rear of the store and laid down on the counter."

Hitt glanced at Lincoln, who had his hands clasped in front of his mouth, taking in Crafton's every word.

"When I went there nobody was in the drugstore but Short and Harrison. They were sitting…on the west side of the drugstore near the front. When I went in and laid down I heard a noise at the door after I had lain there some minutes. I can't cite how long. I raised my head and saw three men in a scuffle. I saw my brother was one and Short and Harrison were the others. I made a spring and got to them. I saw they were in a fight. They met me on the east side of the store about half way… There I met them at the south end of the east counter. As I met them Mr. Short was pulling the boys backwards. He threw out his left hand and caught me. I told him to let him loose, that 'Greek could whip him.'

"He said, 'They shan't fight.' At that they all moved to the southwest on the west side. Here was a counter and by that counter stood some boxes, two or three, two probably. Mr. Harrison being on the east of Greek and Greek on the west of him and Short on the south of the two and me to the south of Short, and we all made a move to the southwest where these boxes were. There my brother fell on those boxes and in this leaning position Mr. Short pushed him backwards over that counter."

He tapped the diagram with the pointer several times to emphasize that position. "That's where I suppose my brother received his stab. I didn't see it. As Mr. Livergood interfered, Mr. Harrison sprang back a foot or two and made a motion to strike my brother again with the knife. Then I jumped over the counter [above it]... Mr. Short moved and I recovered. I jumped between Mr. Harrison and my brother. I threw my right arm to Harrison and he stuck me then with a knife and then jumped over here. I turned and in this position to catch him and he struck at me again. I saw he would use me up with the knife and I made to this east counter over here for the pound weights I knew were always there. As I started I met..." He mumbled a name that Hitt found entirely incomprehensible. As he had been taught, he left the space blank rather than guessing at it.

"...he asked if I was hurt. I replied, 'My God! I am ruined!' I got to where the weights ought to have been, they were not there and I put my hands on the scales and threw them at Harrison. He was hollering, 'Jesus Christ! Have I got no friends here!' As I threw the scales I stumbled against a chair or stool. I picked it up and threw it at him and then turned around and threw two glasses at him. One of them I broke, the other I did not."

At this point, Palmer asked a question. "Had you seen your brother from the time you left him until you saw him engaged in the fight?" His intent was clear: Lincoln was claiming that the Crafton brothers and Livergood had set out that morning to attack Harrison. Palmer was making it clear there had been no such plan. This was a matter of circumstance.

Crafton made that point as he replied. "I saw him at Turley's store, but I didn't speak to him. I was in a hurry and didn't speak to him.

"I went out and left Mr. Harrison in the room after the fight. That is the last I saw of him. I had a pretty bad cut on the right arm in the muscle..." He made a show of attempting to raise his right arm but managed barely more than a few inches. "I have not got the use of it yet. The last I saw of my brother was on the boxes. As I turned I suppose he got up. I saw him next at Dr. Million's. He was then lying on the right side on the floor. I only just passed through the house then. I went to Dr. Million's office and laid down in the shade."

John Crafton paused here and looked down at the floor for several seconds. When he looked up again, he had tears in his eyes. "I never saw my brother again."

12

In the gallery, a chair squeaked. A boot thumped on the floorboard. But the room was otherwise silent.

After a few more questions, Palmer was done with his questioning. Judge Rice looked at the defense table and pointed: your turn.

Slowly, as if burdened by thought, Lincoln rose. He was considered quite skilled at cross-examination. He was known for never asking a question that didn't have a direct purpose. Often that purpose would not become clear till much later.

Lincoln greeted John and began his questions. Lincoln's voice had a heavy tone to it. He asked questions that essentially covered the same ground as the prosecution.

John told about how he looked up when he heard the sound of Greek, Peachy, and Short scuffling. And here Lincoln asked, "About that time did you hear either of the parties say anything?"

"No, sir, I think not. I don't think there was a word spoken. I spoke the first word, I think."

Lincoln looked puzzled, and asked, "You can't remember Harrison saying to your brother that he would not fight or didn't want to fight?"

"No, sir," Crafton said firmly, shaking his head. "I don't remember any such thing. I think I said the first thing spoken in the room. I told Mr. Short to let them loose, that Greek could whip him."

This was not exactly what John Crafton had said to the Grand Jury, Lincoln remembered. So, he asked, "You did not add that Greek *should* whip him?"

"No, sir," Crafton replied, sounding certain. "But I told him he *could* whip him."

Hitt made a mark at the sign for "could." It would remind him to underline it later for emphasis.

Having made his point, Lincoln moved along. With his questioning, John's replies about the timing and the movements, the west, the east, front and back, seemed to become a jumble.

Lincoln kept asking questions in a professorial, non-challenging way. He asked Crafton about everyone's position in relation to the boxes. It seemed to Lincoln that John had not had a clear view of what exactly was happening at the time Greek was stabbed. Lincoln asked casually, but in a firm tone that landed somewhere between a question and a statement, "So you did not see the knife when the blow was given?"

"I did not see the knife go into him."

Lincoln hesitated for a moment. He looked down at his table as if he were examining an invisible document. Then he nodded. The silence was powerful. John Crafton's admission floated slowly through the courtroom: he had not seen the cutting. He was *not* an eyewitness. He did not know, really, when Greek had been stabbed. Was it when his brother was standing up and restraining Harrison or was it when he was falling over the boxes?

Lincoln resumed. "When you first saw the tussle in what way did Quinn and your brother have hold of each other?"

"Well, sir, I could not state exactly for the reason that all three were close together, but I think my brother had his left arm over Quinn's right one. His right one was held by Short."

"You have said Quinn and Greek were face-to-face?"

"They were when I got to them. As I said, they were face-to-face from the time I got to them. They were face-to-face I think all the time."

Lincoln looked puzzled. After seeming to attempt to figure out this dance in his head, he came out from behind his table. His hands were clasped behind him. His gaze was down. Suddenly, he loosened his hands and raised his right index finger, as if the thought had just occurred to him. "Did you see either of them strike at the other with his fist?"

Hitt covered a smile with his palm. He certainly didn't pretend to know the law, but he knew the prime rule of cross-examination: never ask a question to which you don't already know the answer. And Lincoln knew the answer to this question. There had been a lot of testimony on this point already. Greek Crafton was the only one to strike a blow. He hit Peachy Quinn Harrison.

"I think I did," Crafton said, slightly raising his right hand. "I think with this hand. If you will give me a couple of men, I'll show you how it was."

Lincoln turned to face the prosecutor, saying, "I

don't know whether it will do to risk myself, but I'll go in if Mr. Palmer will."

John Palmer agreed.

"I'll make myself Greek," John Crafton said. Unable to use his wounded right arm in this demonstration, Crafton reached up with his left arm and put that hand on Lincoln's shoulder, turning him to face the jury. He placed Palmer at his side, holding one arm. Then he stepped behind Lincoln, where due to Lincoln's size, he was nearly hidden from the jury's sight. Crafton wrapped an arm around Lincoln's body. "They were just this way and I saw Greek make a motion, but whether he hit him or not I could not say. That's the only lick I saw struck."

Lincoln freed himself and faced the witness. "I suppose when you told Short to let him alone, that Greek could whip him, that you had the ordinary meaning and wanted Greek to whip him?"

"I thought after they got into the fight that Greek could whip him."

"And you wanted him to?" There, there it was, Hitt knew.

There was Lincoln throwing the shadow of doubt over Crafton's testimony. Reminding the jurors where his loyalty lay that day—and this day, too.

"Well… I certainly did."

That was Lincoln's final question. John Crafton walked out of the courtroom, the only sound the thump of his boots.

13

The prosecution called a few more witnesses. Daniel Harnett was another young man who had grown up with Greek and Peachy. He testified he went to the drugstore on July 16. He did not see a scuffle between Peachy, Greek, and Mr. Short. He did see that Greek was lying on his side, but he did not know that Greek was injured, let alone stabbed. He also saw Harrison strike John Crafton once with a knife.

On cross-examination by Lincoln, Harnett recalled, "I heard Quinn say something. I think he said, 'My God! Have I no friends here!' I think those were the words he used. I think that was after John had thrown the scales at him, likely he had thrown a stool and the scales too."

Next, Palmer called Frederick Henry to the stand. Henry had been at the Fourth of July picnic where the trouble between Greek and Peachy had started. According to his testimony, by the end of the day, the two young men had put aside their differences.

Hitt glanced at Lincoln. Henry's testimony could be a huge problem for the defense. If Peachy and Greek had made up at the picnic after their harsh words, then there was no reason for Peachy to be afraid. There was no reason for him to borrow a knife in order to defend himself.

Palmer finished his questioning and sat down. Lincoln stood up, ready to repair the damage that had been done. The afternoon heat had been rising in the courtroom. As Lincoln got up, he removed his jacket and placed it over the back of his chair. Lincoln asked Henry about Harrison. "Do you remember his saying at any time that he didn't want to fight?"

Henry nodded vigorously. "He said so, I believe, there when Greek wanted to fight him. I told him, 'We can't have any fighting here.'"

Lincoln nodded his approval. It was a good answer. He asked a final question. Hitt suspected Lincoln asked it less because he really needed the answer but because he wanted to plant a thought in the jury's mind. "Did you hear him say at any time that he, Quinn, was not able to fight Greek?"

"I don't remember that I did."

Lincoln told Judge Rice, "I've got no more questions," and turned to return to his seat. Henry was dismissed.

Hitt had never been in a courtroom that held the heat quite like this one. The windows were opened their full length to catch whatever breezes might sweep through, but the heat was just pouring in. He had taken to mopping his brow regularly. Judge Rice noticed Hitt doing this and asked if he was all right. "I'm fine, your honor. Thank you," Hitt replied.

Judge Rice asked the bailiff to draw the shades, hoping to cut down on the direct sunlight. And then he decided, "Tell you what people. Let's take a little break right here. Why don't you all go 'head and get yourself something to cool down, and we'll see you back here in twenty minutes." Rice gave a single sharp blow of his gavel, and left the stand.

During the afternoon break the courtroom cooled down a bit. When court resumed, Palmer asked that John C. Bone be called next. Bone had seen both

Greek and Peachy at the July Fourth picnic. According to Bone's testimony, later that day Peachy told him about the trouble with Greek. And he showed Bone the knife. With that statement by Bone, Palmer placed the murder weapon in Peachy's hands.

Palmer turned his witness over to Lincoln. Without rising, Lincoln asked, "In that interview between you and Quinn was anything further said?"

"Yes," Bone said, adding in one great rush of speech, "he stated he didn't want to have any difficulty with Crafton and didn't intend to. He might have said it a little further. When he spoke to me about the knife and about Crafton wanting to fight him, I asked him if he wasn't able to fight him, and he said, no, he was not and he had told him he would not fight him and didn't intend to and said if he jumped on him he would hurt him if he could."

Logan then spoke up, clearly attempting to make a strong point from John Bone's testimony. "He was afraid there would be further difficulty?"

"Yes, he was afraid there would be a further difficulty and this knife was a borrowed knife and the man wanted it [back]."

Logan followed up. "He remarked that the man wanted it and he wouldn't have anything to defend himself with?"

"Yes. That's why he said he wanted something of me."

Logan made his point once again, so strongly that Hitt wondered whether to put a question mark or a period on the end. "He wanted something to defend himself with, if he jumped on him?" A question, Hitt decided.

"Yes, sir."

Logan said he was done and Bone made to get up, but Palmer stopped him and asked him to repeat precisely the language Peachy had used. Bone told him, "He said the reason he wanted the knife of me was that that was a borrowed knife and the man wanted it."

"Did he say anything else in that conversation?"

Bone shook his head. "No, sir!"

Hitt knew that Bone, while a witness for the prosecution, had been helpful to the defense. He had testified that Peachy knew of Greek's threats and felt it wise to prepare himself.

Three more witnesses took the stand on behalf of the prosecution. They were Edmund Crafton, who was Greek's uncle, William Graham Purvines, and Peter Livergood. All three were also cross-examined by the defense. Ground was gained and lost by each side. Finally, Palmer thanked everyone for their time and announced that the prosecution was resting its case.

Judge Rice took care of the final business of the

day. He announced that court would reconvene the following morning around nine. Then he reminded the jurors, "Don't you go talking to anybody about anything you heard today, or what's going on in your mind about all this. We got a lot more to hear about this whole issue."

Bang! Court dismissed.

14

The courtroom burst into life. People exhaled. Chairs squeaked. Conversations began. As voices were raised, the noise quickly grew into a near din. At the defense table Lincoln carefully put away his glasses. He neatly packed a few pages into his silk hat. A man who previously had been identified to Hitt as Peyton Harrison, Peachy's father, came forward and leaned over Lincoln's right shoulder. Lincoln turned in his seat and seemed pleased to see him. Logan was talking to Peachy. Palmer walked over to the defense table and said what were obviously some pleasant words to his adversaries. There clearly were no bad feelings between the attorneys on either side.

Hitt closed his inkwells. He cleaned his nibs and put them back in their case. He blotted his latest pages and blew on the ink to help it dry. Then he leaned back and closed his eyes. It had been a long day, made even more difficult by the heat. Hitt paused a moment and took several deep and satisfying breaths before continuing to pack up his workspace. He had filled more than thirty pages with his markings, which would have to be transcribed. There were times he would immediately go to an office and do that work while everything was fresh in his memory. But he had decided that would not be necessary today. He checked his timepiece. It was almost six o'clock.

Coincidently, both he and Lincoln stood at the same time. Lincoln rolled down his sleeves and put on his jacket. After a few words with Logan and young Harrison, Lincoln left the courtroom with Peyton Harrison. He was stopped several times by spectators and exchanged a few words with them, which seemed pleasant enough. Once there was even some light laughter. Then he was gone.

Lincoln headed to his office. Just because the day in court was over, it did not mean that Lincoln was headed home. Trial lawyers spend many hours preparing for each day in court. They also review each day's testimony. And, like most lawyers, Lincoln usually had more than one case at a time.

Herndon was there when Lincoln arrived at the office. He was preparing for several upcoming trials. The two men briefly discussed the events of the day. They both agreed that Palmer had laid out his prosecution professionally, if without much passion. He had demonstrated that Greek had died ugly, from wounds inflicted by Peachy. He had also shown that the Crafton brothers had come unarmed to Short's. Palmer had done his job without leaving any obvious openings for the defense. But that was what the defense team had expected. They knew Palmer. They knew the quality of his lawyering.

As the two men worked, the evening became dark and cooler. A sweet breeze seemingly from nowhere began to push out the heat. The temperature in the office was almost pleasant. Herndon finally finished his work, wished Lincoln a good evening, and went off into the night.

Now alone, Lincoln stretched out on the floor. He leaned against the wall, and allowed his mind to wander through this case. As he once explained, "When I have a particular case in hand, I have that motive and feel an interest…in ferreting out the questions to the bottom, love to dig up the question by the roots and hold it up and dry before the fires of the mind." With past cases, he had found that if he didn't focus on just one point or another, his mind might take him to unexpected places and show him something he hadn't considered before.

As he did sometimes, Lincoln now pulled out his law books. He dived deeper into the law. He forgot the passing time, forgot his family at home. He thumbed through several books, reading more about self-defense.

When he paused, Lincoln glanced around the office. He was unexpectedly struck by a memory. As he had worked this evening, he had focused only on the winning of the case, not the flesh and blood of it. But now Greek Crafton had shown up in his mind.

Lincoln and Herndon had enjoyed having Greek work in their office. He had been a good young man. He had been curious, punctual, and hardworking. Lincoln had believed that Greek would have had a fine career in law, and maybe even in politics. Crafton was certainly smart enough. And his family was well connected, too.

At this moment, Lincoln could recall the sound of Greek's voice and then his laughter, his booming laughter.

Greek had been energetic and cheerful. He often let loose—perhaps too often for Herndon—in long and unrestrained laughter. Some people's laughter barely filled a barrel, but at times the walls of the large office had seemed barely able to contain Greek's laughter.

Lincoln wondered to himself if he was not adequately mourning the loss of young Crafton. He shook his head sadly. It was time to go home.

Palmer and the other prosecuting attorneys had also returned to their office after the day in court. The day had gone well, they agreed. They had made their case without leaving obvious paths for Lincoln and Logan to follow. They believed they had proved that Peachy had carried a knife and killed Greek—an unarmed man—while his own life was in no imminent danger. This would satisfy the legal requirements for both murder and manslaughter.

The experienced Palmer had done an admirable job of preventing any testimony that showed that Harrison had firsthand knowledge of Crafton's threats. Lincoln needed to prove that Harrison knew of those threats in order to prove he had acted in self-defense.

No one on the prosecution team was foolish enough, however, to believe that the case was nearly won. They knew well that the case was only as strong as its weakest part. And they knew that both Lincoln and Logan

ABRAHAM LINCOLN PRESIDENTIAL LIBRARY AND MUSEUM

This photograph from 1859 shows the law offices of John McClernand and Norman Broadwell on the corner of the east side of the public square in Springfield, Illinois.

were experts at finding and exposing any weakness. They wondered where the defense would make their stand the next day.

But no matter what, the prosecution's strategy was set. They would continue to argue that Peachy Quinn Harrison had no reason to arm himself with a deadly weapon. And they would fight tooth and nail to prevent the Reverend Cartwright from repeating Crafton's dying declaration. If it *was* admitted, they would counter it with the testimony of others.

It had been a long but productive day for the four of them. They were pleased to finally put down their work. They wished each other well and walked out into the now pleasant night.

As for Hitt, when he left the courtroom, his hand was throbbing from a full day of writing as quickly as possible. He intended to soak his hand. Instead, he found himself at dinner with James Thomas, another guest at the Globe. The two discussed the trial. They also talked about slavery, the current state of the country, and the possibility of Lincoln running for president. Hitt assured Thomas that Lincoln was a man of great integrity.

"Perhaps there are lawyers who have no problem bending their integrity or belief when necessary," said Hitt, "but his actions during a trial are an accurate reflection of his character."

Thomas then offered his own reading of Hitt's remarks. "So then it makes no difference if his side should win or lose?"

Hitt seemed surprised at that, so surprised he responded with an unusually bold statement. "Oh, of course it does," he said. "Winners win."

15

The next morning, the heat put Judge Rice in a sour mood. So did the thought of spending much of the day arguing the law with Lincoln, Logan, and Palmer. Lincoln may not have been able to cite the statutes by number, but he knew what the law said. And he was never too shy to remind judges of it. Logan often delighted in displaying his own brilliance. And Palmer was a stickler for citations, precedents, and the smallest details of legal history.

Judge Rice stood before a mirror and straightened his robe. He lightly powdered the top of his head to prevent sweat from running down into his eyes and coughed his throat clear. It was time for work. As he settled into his cushioned chair behind the bench and looked out at the overflowing courtroom, he knew for certain this was not going to be a good day to mess with him.

For Hitt, it had already been a busy morning. After a pleasant dinner with Thomas the previous evening, he had returned to his room and worked deep into the night. After only a few hours' rest he had been at the telegraph office when it opened at 6:30 a.m. to send his transcription of yesterday's proceedings to Chicago.

The spectators were still taking their seats when Hitt arrived in the courtroom. There were even more spectators crowding into the room than there had been the previous day. People had even taken seats on the windowsills, their legs dangling in midair.

Suddenly the courtroom began to buzz. Hitt looked up as Harrison and the defense team entered. Lincoln took off his tall hat and began spreading out his papers. He removed his coat and hung it on the back of his chair. Then he rolled up his sleeves. Logan straightened his stack of papers on the table. Harrison, seated at the table, seemed completely lacking in energy. He looked as if he might fall to the floor in a pile if he had to stand up again.

Judge Rice gaveled the court into session. Turning to the defense, he nodded for them to go ahead.

Logan summoned Benjamin Short to the stand. Short, it seemed, had been properly named. In addition to being short in stature, he was stout, and his jowls sagged as if they might be melting in this heat wave. Short acknowledged that he owned a drugstore in Pleasant Plains and was in that store on the morning of July 16.

Logan directed Short, "State when Quinn Harrison came into your store and what followed."

Short scratched his head, demonstrating his commitment to reflection, then recounted, "I think it was about the sixteenth of July at about half-past eight o'clock in the morning he came in. I think the mail had not come in. It was very nearly time for the mail, I remember, when Greek came in. Quinn Harrison was sitting on a stool near the door, I supposed four or five feet from the door inside I should judge. I was sitting side-by-side with him. We were looking over a newspaper, both over the same paper. We remained in that condition until Greek came in."

His testimony almost duplicated the story he had told at the first hearing. Logan urged him to continue, asking, "What then took place? State it all."

"Greek took hold of him the first thing I saw after

he came in. He took hold of Quinn around the arms and the affray [fight] commenced. We rose up immediately, all three of us. Harrison and myself were sitting and rose up and I attempted to separate them. There seemed to be a fight. John Crafton came up. He had come into the store previously. He took hold and we went back together to the rear of the store all hands."

As Short told his story, he began speaking more rapidly. His voice also rose, and he began describing the event with his hands. He waved them about in a growing frenzy. "John took hold of my left arm. I was endeavoring to separate the boys." That last sentence came almost as a plea for understanding. He had tried to stop it. He had tried.

"We all went back together and in going back Harrison got hold of the railing that goes around the counter and was pulled loose from that. He was pulled loose from it by all the other parties, I suppose. John was pulling on me; I was pulling on Greek and pulling on Quinn. He was pulled loose, I think. I think I saw a blow struck by Greek sometime during the affray. I think it was when we had got back to the rear—the back part of the building. I did not notice where he struck him. I did not see when Harrison struck. Greek was between Harrison and me. When John Crafton took hold of me he told me to 'Let him alone, Greek should whip him...'" He paused here, remembering now, his eyes focused on the past. Then he repeated, but this time so softly, "'Greek should whip him.'"

Short looked up, directly at Logan, and continued, "I don't remember anything said when Greek came in and took hold of Harrison." He paused again, and to his own surprise corrected himself. "Yes, Quinn told him he didn't want to fight him and wouldn't fight him—told him to keep off. That was after he took hold of him. Just as he took hold of him."

Logan made sure to emphasize his client's reluctance to fight. He asked, "Did you see Quinn do anything except take hold of the railing?"

"No, sir! I don't know the time the knife was stuck into Greek. I saw Greek striking at Quinn but I don't know where he was stuck. I looked towards the door. There were some men coming and I was anxious for them to get them separated and stopped."

"Did Quinn make any advance to him?" Logan asked. In other words, did Peachy take an offensive or defensive posture?

Short was clear: Peachy made no threatening moves. "Greek took hold of him before he got up. He commenced raising just as Greek took hold of him. Greek went right to Harrison and took hold of him right straight. I think he didn't say anything." He shook his head. "I don't recollect. He had his coat off. I could not say whether he had his hat off. I didn't see him pull it off. It was possibly off when he came through the door."

Then it came to him in a snap. "He pulled it off and threw it down and made right at Harrison before he began to rise. What Harrison said was just about the time he took hold of him—about his not wanting to fight him." Logan looked at Lincoln and sat down.

Lincoln stood and removed his glasses. "Mr. Short," he began, "where was John Crafton when the difficulty commenced with Quinn?"

"He was in the back part of the building. He had been there a very short time—I could not say just how long."

"He had been in more than once that morning?" The point Lincoln was trying to make was that the Crafton brothers had been waiting for Harrison. Maybe even laying a trap for him.

"I don't know. I don't know what he was doing there."

"Did he say anything about having come because he expected somebody to leave money for him?"

"He did not to my recollection."

Lincoln paused, allowing the jurors to take that in. It was not what John Crafton had testified. Then, just to make certain jurors understood, he asked with mock surprise, "He did not ask you if anybody had left money with you, and finally have some talk that it might have been left with Mr. Hart?"

Short was definite about it. "I don't recollect anything of it. I don't recollect any talk between him and me about money at all."

Lincoln next asked, "Which counter did Quinn hold onto by the rail?"

"The east counter on the east side of the room."

"You have not told what happened after Greek was cut?"

Short nodded. He knew what Lincoln was referring to. "After they were separated John Crafton threw some scales and some glasses and a stool at Harrison. John got cut somehow in the scrape. I did not see that. After they were separated and Quinn and Greek got apart Quinn kept pretty close to the rear of the store, I think in one corner near as I can recollect. He kept his ground and John threw at him. He asked if he had no friends here, I don't recollect whether he said it more than once but I recollect hearing him say that once. He asked if he had no friends there."

"Did he make at anybody after the separation from Greek?"

"No, I think not."

"Or at any other time?"

"No, sir, I think not. I didn't see him make at anybody during the whole affair."

Lincoln pushed harder at the idea that Harrison was always defending himself by asking, "As he went down did anyone push him?"

"They dragged him down," Short said, his whole manner an accusation. "They, the Crafton brothers, working together, dragged him to the ground."

Lincoln asked a significant question that called for Short to state his opinion, as the fact could not be known. "Which was the larger and stronger man of the two?"

Palmer did not object. "I think Greek was the largest considerably if there was any difference. The strongest man also, I think."

Logan and Lincoln sat, satisfied.

16

Palmer stood and acknowledged with a pleasant nod the fine job done by the opposition. "Mr. Short," Palmer began, indicating the diagram of the store. "You observe an imperfect sort of figure here on the floor meant to represent your store. Describe it."

"Yes." Short proceeded to repeat the explanation given previously, adding little to it beyond a guess that the store ran thirty feet deep. He also agreed he was about four or five feet from the front door when Greek entered. Palmer asked him what he was doing when Greek came in. "Looking over a newspaper," he said.

"Greek's step on the door first attracted my attention. I suppose I stopped reading. I might have commenced again. It's a mere matter of impression."

Palmer had a calm and reassuring way about him as he asked the defense witness his questions. There was no suggestion he was challenging Short's memory of the events. Rather he was simply attempting to clarify them. "Was your attention attracted to Harrison as Greek came in?"

"Yes, when he took hold of him. I think not until then. He was sitting as close to me as he could when Greek took hold of him. I think both of us were leaning against the counter. It's about the usual height of counters. We were sitting on stools and leaning against the counter. When my attention was first attracted to Harrison, Crafton had not taken hold of him. I saw him before he took hold of him. I think Harrison was still leaning against the counter."

"Did you apprehend any difficulty?"

"No, sir. Not until it commenced. In passing he passed along the usual passage way."

"Then he was approaching you as well as Harrison when you first observed him?"

"Yes," Short answered, but with less conviction than previously, clearly wondering if Palmer was leading him into some clever trap.

"When did you make up your mind that there was going to be a fight?"

"As soon as I discovered him taking off his coat. It was just as he stepped into the house [store]."

Palmer considered that long enough for the jurors to understand he was considering it. Then he asked, "Wasn't there plenty of time for you to have placed yourself between them?"

The sarcasm in Short's answer showed he did not appreciate the question. "I suppose I might have put myself between them—if I had been in a pretty smart hurry." For the first time he looked to the gallery for support. The spectators were listening intently. No support came.

"Did he walk or rush in?"

"He walked in passing."

"Did Harrison observe him taking off his coat?"

Short pursed his lips. "I don't know. I don't think he said anything. I suppose the noise Crafton made drew his attention."

"Do you know any reason why it should not?" At that moment Palmer's purpose became clear to many in the courtroom. He wanted to make certain the jurors understood that Harrison was not surprised and taken. In fact, Harrison was aware of Crafton's presence and had sufficient opportunity to defend himself.

Judge Rice leaned back. His sour mood was lightened. So much time in a courtroom was filled with nonsense, he thought. Often his most difficult task was fighting to stay awake when overwhelmed by boredom. But watching smart lawyers do their business was still a treat for him. Lincoln, Logan, and Palmer were putting on a fine show.

"I don't know. I am very apt to look up when I hear steps at the door."

As friendly as can be, Palmer asked the witness, "Is it not true that as Crafton came up Harrison rose to his feet?"

Short was confused, but tried sticking to his story. "He rose to his feet when Crafton took hold of him. I don't think he did before."

"Did not Crafton take hold of him just about the time he was rising?"

"About that time, he did."

"Did you observe Crafton take hold of him as he was rising?"

Short paused once again. The timing was getting a little confusing. He tried to remember exactly how he had told it before, but he couldn't be certain. "I don't think I did," he said, the conviction now gone from his voice.

"Did you observe whether Harrison's hands were or were not about his bosom as he was rising?"

"I did not. I don't think I observed more than his turning his face from him. He had hold of him at that time, or he was taking hold of him about that time." He felt on firmer ground, repeating that this was about the time Harrison said loudly that he did not want to fight.

Palmer took that opportunity to remind the jurors of Peachy's threats. "Did he say to Crafton that if he laid hands on him he would kill him?"

"I think not," Short said, but Palmer had gotten his work done. That reminder could not be unheard. Short continued, "Nothing about killing or defending himself I think. I think he said he didn't want to fight or wouldn't fight to keep him off."

Palmer turned his back on the witness and faced the jury as he asked, "Was the tone of his voice loud or moderate?"

"I don't recollect."

"Did he curse Crafton?"

"He did not."

He turned around then and faced Short, asking, "That's all you recollect?"

"Yes."

Palmer then took Short through the fight again,

questioning the smallest details. Palmer asked question after question about pushing and directions and distances, east and west and front and back, enough to confuse even the brightest juror.

By this time, Hitt's thumb was throbbing. He picked up a thinner pen, trying to move its resting place to a different spot on his thumb in order to reduce the aching. That was about all he could do.

Palmer continued snapping questions at Short, leaving him as little space as possible to gather his thoughts.

The cross-examination was impressive. Palmer managed to raise doubts about the accuracy of Short's memory, while suggesting quite a different interpretation of the facts.

Palmer had moved his case forward small steps at a time. Lincoln and Logan had permitted that without interruption, as it had no bearing on their fundamental contention that Peachy had acted in self-defense.

But then Palmer crossed the line. He asked, "Did you see any sign of any particular danger to anybody or regard Harrison as in any danger of any immediate injury?"

"Objection!" Lincoln and Logan rose as one. This went right to the heart of their case. If Harrison had sensed no danger, he would not have had reason to strike out with his knife.

Neither lawyer stated the reason for their objection. It was not necessary in that courtroom. However, it was clear that this question called for the witness to state his own unqualified opinion. Most times opposing attorneys would allow it, but it was a risk they could not take.

Judge Rice agreed. "Sustained."

Palmer asked a few more questions and then the defense followed up with a few of their own. Finally, Short was dismissed.

Hitt quickly flexed his fingers and leaned back. Then he glanced a look at Lincoln. Lincoln was not a man who allowed any show of emotion, but Hitt thought he detected the edges of a satisfied smile.

17

The defense called Dr. John Allen to the stand. On the morning of July 16, Dr. Allen had business at Short's drugstore. He arrived there after the brawling had begun. But what he had seen that day was not the reason his testimony was so important to the defense. They were more interested in what he had *heard*.

Stephen Logan asked him, "Did you see the whole or any part of the scrape between Quinn Harrison and Greek Crafton on the sixteenth of July?"

"I saw some of it," Dr. Allen said. "I didn't see the first commencement of it."

"State what you saw," Logan asked. "Did you go there with the expectation of seeing anything? Did you hear Greek Crafton make any threats before on that day?"

Palmer was up quick as a shot to object. He said there should be no testimony allowed about threats supposedly made, unless it could be shown that Harrison himself knew about the threats before the fight.

Threats are made easily and often, Palmer contended. There may have been many threats made, but in this trial they had no relevance unless it could be proved that Harrison had direct knowledge of them. Jurors could not presume that he had knowledge of them. They could not make that connection through circumstance. It had to be proved with evidence that Harrison was directly and personally aware of the threats. Then and only then could it be argued that he got himself the knife with the white handle.

They had reached the heart of the defense's case.

Palmer was standing. Logan was standing. Lincoln stood.

Judge Rice instructed the bailiff to remove the jury for this argument.

Hitt laid down his pen. The whole of this legal discussion was not to be transcribed, just the gist of it.

Palmer spoke first. He made a strong legal argument. The jury was being asked to consider the defendant's state of mind when he committed the stabbing and therefore was entitled to hear only those *facts* that might have influenced him. Whether or not Crafton made threats was not relevant. There were no facts or evidence to prove that Harrison had been aware of Crafton's words. It was all hearsay.

Palmer argued vigorously for several minutes pointing out the obvious: Greek Crafton could not be present in the courtroom to confirm or deny that he had actually spoken those words. And while he held great respect for Dr. Allen, the law on hearsay was clear. It was not admissible in this instance.

Palmer also stated that even if those words *had* been uttered, without Crafton's testimony there was no way to know what he had truly meant by them. The same words might be spoken in all seriousness or in complete jest. A phrase as simple as, "I did it," takes on a completely different meaning when said as a statement—"I did it!"—than when asked as a question—"I did it?" It is not right, Palmer cautioned, to assign a meaning to a dead man's words that might not be what he had intended. Particularly on something this important.

It was a strong argument, Lincoln acknowledged as he commended Mr. Palmer for his thoughtful presentation. But he reckoned it had little bearing on this argument. It was not only Peachy Harrison's state of mind that Logan desired to demonstrate to the jury, but also that of Greek Crafton. Was it not necessary to determine Crafton's motive? Clearly, if Crafton started the fight with the intent to gravely injure Harrison, it made Harrison's need to resist that much more persuasive. And the only way to show that was through Crafton's own words.

Hitt was taken by the change in Lincoln as he argued his points. He noticed a distinct shift from the folksy, almost breezy Lincoln when the jury was present to the more formal attorney now presenting a legal argument. Rather than standing behind his table, he moved around the courtroom as he made his points. At first his hands were locked behind his back. Gradually, he began to poke at the air with his right hand to emphasize a point. His voice remained firm and strong. He commanded the courtroom so totally it was not necessary to raise it.

Lincoln roamed the courtroom making his plea, reminding Judge Rice that the law might be flexible on such points, and with a young man's life in the balance it was far better to follow the spirit of the law rather than be held hostage to a strict interpretation. Let him have his best defense, Lincoln pleaded. As his arguments continued, Hitt was struck by Lincoln's obvious respect for his words. People liked to call him plainspoken, but what Hitt noticed was Lincoln's ability to string ordinary words together in a way that made people pause and think about them in a different light.

If the courthouse truly was "dedicated to the cause of justice," Lincoln continued, then this must be the proper way to conduct the business of the law.

Logan followed him, pursuing the legal argument with skill. He told Judge Rice that the defense intended to satisfy Palmer's objections by putting additional witnesses on the stand who would testify that Harrison had indeed been made aware of the threats. Allen's testimony would be confirmed by those men.

Judge Rice took pride in allowing defendants as much opportunity as was legal to make their strongest argument. He had enjoyed this debate. It was a fine legal argument. It reminded him of the reason he had chosen the law so many years earlier. And, for just a few moments, he had been so enmeshed in it that he forgot the maddening heat.

Logan's promise about additional testimony had helped him make his decision. Judge Rice announced, "There has to be evidence that the prisoner had knowledge of these threats before the fight and this testimony doesn't satisfy. Therefore the objection is sustained."

The jury was brought back in. When everyone was

settled, the questioning resumed. Both Lincoln and Palmer asked Dr. Allen about what he had seen. He'd seen the struggle, but he hadn't seen a knife. "I never saw a knife that day," he said. But he did hear John Crafton say loudly, "Let him have it," and "Give it to him." He heard him say it a few times, "as quick as he could," although he could not remember how often he had repeated those words.

Skinny Thomas White followed Dr. Allen onto the stand. White had been at the Fourth of July picnic. Logan took him through the questioning to try to prove that Harrison knew of Greek's threats. White testified that he himself heard Greek say that he intended to whip Harrison.

Logan asked, "Did you tell that to Quinn Harrison?" White nodded firmly. "I told Quinn Harrison I heard a man say he was going to whip him there that day. I don't know as I told him it was Mr. Crafton, but I knew he knew it was Crafton soon as I spoke."

After more questioning, Palmer did his cross-examination and then White was dismissed. As he left the courtroom a few of his pals gave him a hearty slap on his back. White's testimony had served the defense well. He left the jurors with the impression that a larger, stronger man had been bullying a smaller one. Good people understood that sometimes a man could be pushed too far. And it was accepted that a man had a right to defend himself from being pummeled by a much bigger man.

To reinforce this notion the defense called Dr. Albert Atherton. He testified that he considered Harrison "to be a man of feeble health and strength."

Logan asked Dr. Atherton if Harrison was too weak to work. Being too weak to work was a concept understood, and feared, by the men of Sangamon County. A man had to work to survive. Everyone knew that.

Dr. Atherton answered, "I think, sir, he has not been able to make a hand at any ordinary labor…for at least the past two years."

It became apparent to Hitt that just about everyone in the courtroom was stealing a glance or two at the defendant. Harrison had no doubt been made ready for this. He sat calmly in his seat and kept his eyes on Logan.

To Hitt, Harrison looked slight. His shirt sagged on his shoulders. His exposed arms were thin without much indication of biceps. His complexion was pale. His appearance gave no suggestion of any type of strength—physical, mental, or emotional.

When it was the prosecution's turn, Palmer questioned Dr. Atherton about how often he had treated Harrison.

"I don't recollect," Dr. Atherton admitted. Then he added, "Several times. I was called to treat him first for pneumonia, or inflammation of the lungs, that was probably four years ago. He has had several attacks of the same since that one. I don't recollect what was the matter with him at the time he was unable to do road labor. He was not quite so well then as usual, I think."

That was Palmer's last question. Dr. Atherton stood to his full height and walked out of the courtroom.

18

Lincoln called the Reverend Peter Cartwright to the stand. Finally. This was the witness the spectators had been waiting for.

The reverend walked with the aid of a lion's-head cane to the stand. He wore a black jacket, black vest, white shirt, and the wide black band of his profession around his neck, covered in part by a white collar. Lincoln sat ramrod straight as Cartwright walked by him and took the stand. The two men did not look at each other.

There was some isolated applause that was stopped quickly by Judge Rice. While it wasn't often the judge

Reverend Peter Cartwright, Peachy Quinn Harrison's grandfather and a witness for the defense.

had a real celebrity in his courtroom, he wasn't about to allow any improper behavior. "None of that in my courtroom, please. This is a place of justice, not a meeting, and we'll have none of that," he exclaimed. Then he glanced at the witness and acknowledged him pleasantly, "Reverend."

"Judge," Cartwright responded.

The anticipation in the courtroom almost made people forget about the heat. For nearly three decades Lincoln and Cartwright had found precious little in common. But now the fate of Peachy Quinn Harrison had brought them together.

Like everyone else in the courtroom, Hitt looked from one to the other. Reverend Cartwright looked down as he tried to make himself comfortable in the hard wooden witness chair. He avoided looking at Lincoln. And Lincoln avoided looking at the reverend. He busied himself leafing through papers.

While Hitt could not know this for sure, he assumed that Cartwright, Lincoln, and Logan had met before this moment. They must have gotten together to discuss Cartwright's testimony. It would have been an uncomfortable meeting, for sure. But the stakes for Peachy were so high. Lincoln and Cartwright would have tried to be polite and set aside their differences long enough to achieve their shared goal of getting Harrison acquitted.

Hitt imagined the meeting as brief and formal. Logan undoubtedly explained to Cartwright the challenges in getting Judge Rice to even allow his testimony. Then Lincoln might have taken him through the basic issues point by point. Hitt envisioned that at the end of the meeting Lincoln and Cartwright might have shaken hands—and later both of them would have washed well.

★ ★ ★

After much deliberation and discussion, the defense team had decided that Logan should do the questioning. Disappointed, spectators watched as Logan rather than Lincoln stood to face the witness.

"Have you, Dr. Cartwright, been pretty well acquainted in the family of Mr. Harrison, particularly with Quinn?"

The years of preaching the Lord's word in the forests and prairies had taken their toll on the reverend's voice. His voice was scratchy, and he had to speak as loudly as he could in order to be heard at the back of the courtroom.

"Yes, sir. Ever since he was an infant."

"State the reason of your being so particularly acquainted." The defense believed it was better to get this relationship out on the table rather than pretend it was less than it was.

"Well, sir, he is my grandson, my eldest daughter's son."

"You have been about the house a good deal, Mr. Cartwright?"

"Oh yes, and he has been about my house frequently, often."

Logan stayed in place behind his table, to ensure that Cartwright had the full attention of the jurors.

"Do you know anything about his health for several years past?"

"Yes, sir. I think I know very well."

Lincoln, aware that spectators might be watching him to gauge his reaction, remained as still as possible. His clasped hands rested in front of him on the table.

Logan asked Cartwright to describe his grandson's ill health, "in your own way."

After clearing his throat, Cartwright said, "Well, he was…"

He paused and appealed to Mr. Logan, "If I commence wrong set me right. Quinn was a very healthy child, as I understand it, for a good many years. He was an active, busy boy, surprisingly so for his age. But his health began to decline and I considered he was employed in too much business for his health, and I remonstrated with his father on the subject. His father had perceived it himself, and he relaxed from what he had formerly required of him. I know of my own certain knowledge, that for a good many years he has been a sickly puny boy, not able to do what we would call common manual labor."

Logan continued to make his point, asking, "Was there anything that called your attention to the propriety of his doing any work in which the state of his health was at risk?"

"Well, I considered that it was improper for him to do ordinary work in the business of the farm."

"That was on account of the state of his health?"

The preacher cleared his throat once again. "Yes, sir, his health has been very feeble, often laid up, and sometimes in the course of that time he was sick nigh unto death."

And then, without changing his tone at all, Logan changed the subject. He said to Cartwright, "State whether you were with Greek Crafton, shortly before he died, and at the time he was expecting death, and if so, state what you heard, if you heard anything."

That brought Palmer to his feet. He objected loudly. "Dying declarations are not admissible evidence, your Honor, and Mr. Logan is well aware of that."

Logan reminded Palmer and the court that this was not true. He pointed out that given specific circumstances, the confessions of men on their deathbed *had* often been deemed admissible. It was up to the judge to decide.

Lincoln remained silent and seated as Logan and Palmer made their respective points. Judge Rice declared that he found no simple answer in the law. He decided that in order for him to determine if this part of Cartwright's testimony could be allowed, he needed to hear it in its entirety. So the jury would have to leave the courtroom, he said. They should not hear this part of Cartwright's testimony unless, after the judge heard it, he decided it was admissible.

19

Now Lincoln stood up and took the lead. Although he had great respect for the bench, he said, he didn't understand why Judge Rice needed to know exactly what was said in order to determine if a man's dying declaration could be heard in court.

Lincoln wanted to know what standard the judge intended to apply when making his decision. What words would make it too strong for the jury to hear? This was a classic Lincoln legal strategy: make an argument in the form of a question.

Judge Rice gave his reply. If they proceeded, as Lincoln seemed to be suggesting, and the testimony turned out to be tainted, he would have to declare a mistrial. Then there would have to be a new trial and everything would have to be done again, starting from the beginning. He was quite certain Lincoln didn't want that any more than he did. So the best course of action was for him to hear all of Cartwright's testimony about what Greek said on his deathbed, first, and then decide if it was admissible.

In later years, the issue of admissibility most likely would have been settled long before Cartwright was even called to the stand. But the standards that would eventually become common in trials were still evolving.

Judge Rice decided this was a good time for a lunch break. He ordered the bailiff to take the jurors out and make sure they all got something to eat. Then he banged hard twice on the sound block to put the court in recess.

When the session resumed, the courtroom felt odd with the jury box sitting empty. But things got underway quickly as Logan continued with the questioning. "Go on, Mr. Cartwright, and tell the story," he urged.

Cartwright nodded, and began. "I understand that this affray [fight] took place July 16. I was not at home, nor present at the time." He looked at Palmer and said,

"I know nothing of the quarrel, pro or con, except by hearsay. I was friendly to all the parties, in good friendship and fellowship as far as I know."

He returned his attention to Logan. "I passed through the village where this affray took place on my return from some lower counties home, obtained my papers and letters from the post office and heard not a word about this affray until I got home. When I entered the room, my wife asked me if I had heard of the dreadful affair. I told her, 'No, not a word.' When she repeated it, it shocked me exceedingly."

For the first time his gaze slid just a bit and appeared to fix on his grandson and Lincoln. He cleared his throat then continued, "A day or two before this my horse had fallen upon me, and crippled me in my right hip. The day was exceedingly hot, and I was exceedingly faint, and sick. In a few minutes a messenger from the village, Mr. James Fanes, came in, saying that Greek Crafton, who was wounded, had sent for me to pray for him.

"I did not know how I was to get there. I had turned my horse into the pasture and I had no one to catch him, but he said he had brought a wagon and I could ride up. I thought, at first, I could not go, I was faint and weary: but I concluded to make the effort, and went.

"When I came to the village, I learned that he was

at the house of his brother-in-law, Dr. Million. I made my way to the house and went into the room. It was considerably crowded and all present were affected; I was affected myself, deeply and solemnly too, for I had heard that it was supposed that the wound was mortal."

The reverend's voice seemed to gain strength as he went on. But his eyes seemed slowly to lose their focus on the courtroom as his mind drifted back into the past. "The wounded young man, Greek Crafton was lying on a little trundle bed that was near the floor, and I, not being able to stoop on account of the injury to my hip, I knelt down by his bedside and took him by the hand and expressed my deep regret and sorrow that this fatal calamity had fallen upon him—for I looked upon it as fatal from what I heard on all sides. I looked upon him as in a dying condition and felt accordingly. When I took him by the hand and thus expressed my deep sorrow he said, I think at that moment, 'The honest hour has come, and in a few moments I expect to stand before my final judge; do you think there are any mercy for me? Will you pray for me?'"

Palmer sat back and let Cartwright have his complete say. With the jury out of the courtroom there was no damage to be done to his case by this testimony, and even he was touched by the aching tone in Cartwright's words.

"I then repeated my regret and sorrow at the circumstance, the fatal stab that I supposed he had received. I expressed my deep and heartfelt regret that this calamity had fallen upon him. He paused a moment and made this reply, I think literally, 'Yes,' said he, 'I have brought it upon myself, and I forgive Quinn,' or 'Quinn Harrison.' I am not certain which, he seemed as calm and composed as any man could possibly have been in his situation, and I really wondered that he could command himself as he did. He requested religious services, and we went through them as best we could over a dying man. I have visited hundreds of dying fellows and I thought I never saw a man in a dying condition more calm and composed, more perfectly than himself."

Hitt could not recall ever being brought so strongly into a past moment by a witness. His craft had enabled him to perfect the art of dispassion, but here he saw the courage of the boy and felt it. He kept his head buried in his work so as not to show any of the emotion he was feeling.

Cartwright shook his head in sadness. "His mind seemed to be entirely fixed on his final destiny and not on the sympathetic wailings of his friends around him. I then arose, being in extreme pain from my crippled hip, and it being extremely warm, stepped back two or three feet, not very distant. There were two doors to the room, to the north and south, and on the east and west windows that were hoisted. I stepped back to get the air. A lady handed me a seat; I sat down to get the benefit of the air, to relieve myself. Then I heard him repeat distinctively what he had said to me, 'I have brought it upon myself. I forgive Quinn and I want it said to all my friends that I have no enmity [hatred] in my heart against any man, and if I die…'

"Previous to this, at the close of the services, he had said that he hoped for mercy from a final judge. '…If I die, I want it declared to all that I die in peace with God and all mankind.' I sat there in my pain. I cannot tell how long. I think I got through between one and two o'clock. I am not certain as to the time. I lingered there two or three hours. The room being crowded and the doctor not able under the circumstances to keep it clear for a free circulation of air, I requested the doctor to do so, for that was enough to kill the dying man, if nothing else. I then removed outside to the shade, for the sun was getting pretty low and soon returned home. That is the substance of what I can recollect."

The reverend settled back in the seat, done. He took a handkerchief from an inner pocket and wiped his brow. Then he looked up at Judge Rice, as if to ask if more was needed. Judge Rice looked to Logan and Lincoln to see if they had further questions. They did not. "Mr. Palmer?" he asked.

Palmer shook his head. "No, your Honor."

Judge Rice said pleasantly, "Thank you, Pastor, thank you very much. Please stay around here a bit."

The courtroom, quiet until now, breathed a collective sigh. All the restrained noise was let loose at once. It seemed like everyone had something to say about Cartwright's testimony. Judge Rice let it go on for a bit. He appeared to be busy straightening up his bench, but he really was considering his decision. Finally he picked up his gavel. It took him four hits to silence the room. "Quiet down!" he yelled. "Let's quiet it down."

Kidd, too, tried to clamp down the noise, shouting, "Quiet down, just quiet down."

Judge Rice fidgeted on the bench. He scratched his head, deciding how to proceed. Hitt looked at Harrison, who sat rock still at the table. His eyes were locked on the judge.

20

Judge Rice cleared his throat. He knew the stakes here, he said. He wanted to make sure the defendant got a fair shake. Then he began to speak about the law, saying it was set down by men to bring order to a chaotic world. It occurred to Hitt that the judge was fumbling his way along, trying to figure out, while he spoke, how he wanted to rule. The judge pointed out that since the law had been made by man, then every single soul in the courtroom knew for sure it wasn't going to be perfect.

Then he began to explain that where dying declarations were concerned, previous courts had seemed to find a significant difference between statements of fact and statements of opinion. Exceptions to the hearsay rule had most often been acceptable when a dying person had provided important information about the cause of their demise. Who had done it, for example, or how it had been done. But that was not the situation here, he said. There wasn't much dispute about any of that. And try as he might, he didn't see how this qualified…

A sudden motion to his left startled Hitt. With no warning, Lincoln erupted. He sprang from his chair and demanded, in a massive voice that rattled the courtroom walls, "Your honor! We need to see this through. Every last bit of it!"

Hitt was stunned. He had never seen such an unexpected explosion of passion in his life. Lincoln clearly had heard Judge Rice drifting toward ruling the evidence out. He was determined to stop the judge before he reached that end.

Lincoln was at the bench in the wink of an eye. The calm manner in which Lincoln had previously conducted himself was gone. It was replaced by a controlled fury. This ruling could not be allowed to stand, he insisted. The words seemed to burst out of him. The law was not a game to be played, he thundered, as he now roamed the courtroom. His unleashed energy was making it impossible for him to remain still.

Justitia, Lady Justice, has carried her scale in one hand since the time of the Roman Emperors, he said. It was a reminder that *all* the evidence must be weighed. All of it! It was not the job of the court, he yelled, shaking his index finger to emphasize that point, not the job of the court to push down the scales on one side. Rather, the court needed to make certain that every last bit of grain is counted. Then, and only then, will the balance of justice be done.

He pointed to the prosecution table. "Those are able people sitting there, your honor," he said. He knew them all. He knew how good they were. The last thing they needed or wanted was the court's help to fix their case, Lincoln declared. They've got their own things to say about this, so let it all be heard, every word of it. Then let the jury give it the appropriate weight.

Later, Hitt would describe the scene to a reporter. "Lincoln sprang to his feet and he seemed to be going right over the top of the bench on top of the judge. I never saw a demonstration of power manifested in any human being in my life equal to that."

This was an aspect of Lincoln's character Hitt had not seen before. It was stirring. He was forceful and determined, his usually measured words were dripping with emotion. He was attacking Judge Rice with a mixture of logic and law.

"It was," Captain Kidd would later recall, "a display of anger, the like of which I never saw exhibited by him before or after."

Lincoln went on this way for several minutes. Hitt thought that at times Lincoln came close to contempt of court. But Judge Rice allowed him to continue. Lincoln finished by saying that the deceased had a right to be heard. Then he sat down.

Judge Rice glared at him. "You finished?"

"I am, your honor. Thank you."

Judge Rice turned to address the gallery. "As I was saying before Mr. Lincoln found it necessary to give us all the benefit of his learned opinion…" He then proceeded to explain that he couldn't see how the Reverend Cartwright's testimony qualified under the dying declaration exception. But he also didn't see how he could exclude it fairly, especially since the prosecution was ready to offer powerful rebuttal witnesses.

On balance, he said, looking at Lincoln with an almost sarcastic smile, he saw more damage potentially being done by excluding this testimony than by allowing it. So for that reason he had decided to let the jury hear it.

"Thank you, your honor," Lincoln said, but his

words were lost. Once again, the courtroom erupted. Lincoln cupped his hands around Quinn Harrison's ear and said something, to which Harrison nodded vigorously. For the first time in the whole trial, Peachy smiled.

21

The judge's ruling surprised Hitt, but of course he didn't show it. Judge Rice had seemed well on his way to announcing a different decision. But Lincoln had seemingly turned him around. Of course, Hitt had no way of knowing if Judge Rice really *had* been persuaded by Lincoln to change his mind or if he was always going there. It didn't matter. The result was the same: the jury would be permitted to hear the victim apparently taking the blame for his own death, excusing the accused.

Before he recalled the jury, Judge Rice asked Palmer if he wanted to say anything. Palmer said he accepted the decision. But he asked that Cartwright's testimony be confined strictly to his declarations as to the facts of the killing. He knew, of course, that this would effectively gut Cartwright's testimony.

Palmer argued that most of the testimony was irrelevant. He couldn't recall any part of the criminal statutes that said it mattered if the victim forgave the accused. Under the law, he said, the heart of the testimony should be ruled inadmissible.

Logan spoke for the defense. He argued that this went directly to the state of Greek Crafton's mind when he started the fight. The jury had the right to know that Greek had set out to beat Harrison.

Lincoln spoke next. Now calm, he spoke briefly and well about the right of the accused to present his best defense. He called it fundamental to the concept of a trial by a jury of your peers.

Judge Rice overruled Palmer's objection. He told the bailiff to get the jury. When the jury had been reseated, Judge Rice told them he was going to let them hear what the Reverend Cartwright had to say. He also told them that they better pay close attention. There were still some parts of this testimony that he might later decide they shouldn't consider in their deliberations.

The Reverend Cartwright sat back in the witness

chair. This being such an unusual occurrence, no one knew quite how to proceed. Logan shrugged and told him he might just as well go ahead and tell the whole story over again. The Reverend chuckled to himself and admitted, "I don't know but these lawyers have got me so tangled up that I don't know which end of me is up, but I will try to be as collected as I still can. If I understand myself, I am now to repeat what I have said once?"

Cartwright was encouraged to go through his entire testimony again. And so he did. He told of passing through the village and of his horse falling. He told about being summoned to Greek's bedside. He recalled Greek's words… But then, as before, he stared into the past and repeated Greek's words with real pain in his voice. "Will you pray for me?"

"I have no enmity [hatred] in my heart." And, finally, "I die in peace with God and all mankind."

When he finished this second telling, he coughed a few times.

Judge Rice asked the prosecution if they had any questions for the reverend. Palmer said they did not. Everyone including Hitt was taken aback by this. *No* questions? This suggested that the prosecution did not believe the Reverend Cartwright had really damaged their case. In addition, they probably didn't want to risk alienating the jury by attacking such a respected, beloved figure. Better to release him and use other witnesses to refute his testimony.

Cartwright was discharged. As he walked slowly across the courtroom, he cocked his head, caught Lincoln's gaze, and nodded with satisfaction.

22

Madison Cartwright testified next for the defense. The twenty-four-year-old was the eldest of the Reverend Cartwright's eight children. He had been present for Greek's deathbed conversation with the reverend. He testified, "I heard Greek say this, 'I brought it upon myself.'"

That was all Lincoln asked and the prosecution waved him off without asking a single question.

Next called was P. M. Carter, another young man of Sangamon County who had known both Crafton and Harrison. He testified that a week or so before the fight, Greek told him he intended to fight with Peachy. This happened in Turley's store.

Lincoln asked Carter, "Previous to the affray did you tell Quinn of that?"

"I cannot say that I did." Carter sighed, trying to dredge up a memory that would not come. "But it seems to run in my mind that I did. But I can't refresh my mind of any time or place."

Lincoln found that curious. "It seems to run in your mind," he repeated, "but you can't be certain about it?"

Reaching the truth required a nifty twist of the language. "Yes, I can't," Carter answered.

Lincoln responded in kind. "You was not there on the sixteenth?"

"No, sir!"

After a brief break, the trial resumed and the defense called the Reverend John Slater. Slater had ministered to Crafton throughout most of his final ordeal. He confirmed what Greek had told the Reverend Cartwright: Crafton said he had brought it all upon himself and that he forgave Peachy.

Lincoln recognized the perfect place to stop. There was nothing that he could get from this witness that would be more helpful.

So he thanked him, glanced at Mr. Palmer and said, "John."

"Thank you, Abe," Palmer said. Palmer asked Slater a few questions. He asked if Slater recalled anything else Greek had said about Peachy's connection with his death.

"I think not that I recollect."

Palmer persisted. He was looking for something more.

"Do you recollect any further allusion to Harrison?"

"No, sir. No allusion to Mr. Harrison."

Palmer finally asked, "Do you recollect any remark about his being held while Harrison stabbed him?"

Throughout the courtroom people suddenly sat taller. "No, sir," Slater said flatly.

"Do you remember Mr. Short's name being used?"

"No, sir, not at that time."

Palmer stood directly in front of the witness. He remained standing, waiting to see if the witness would add anything more. Silence tends to make witnesses uneasy. They will often react by rushing to fill the silence with more words than they had intended. In this instance, however, the Reverend Slater remained quiet. Finally Palmer said, "Thank you" and turned away. The very question was intended to suggest that instead of slashing out at an attacking Crafton in self-defense, Harrison had purposefully taken hold of Crafton and stabbed him. That possibility was now floating in the air.

Tom Turley, the owner of Turley's store, was next. His testimony reinforced that of others who had been in his store when Greek threatened to hurt Peachy. He also repeated the fact that Greek was larger and stronger than Peachy.

Palmer's cross-examination was brief.

The trial had picked up rhythm as the defense built its case piece by piece. Dr. John Allen, who had not been allowed to testify about threats he might have heard during his previous appearance in the witness box, was recalled to the stand for more questions. Judge Rice reminded him that he was still under oath.

"Nice to see you ag'in." Lincoln said, finally able to ask the witness, "If, at any time after the fourth of July and before the actual encounter on the sixteenth between these parties, you heard Greek Crafton say anything about Quinn Harrison, tell where, when and what it was."

Dr. Allen nodded that he understood the question, and that he had something to say about that. "It was the day it happened," he said. "It was early in the morning."

"How long before the affray took place?"

"I can't say positive how long. It was not more than half an hour, I suppose."

"Where was it?"

Dr. Allen had been waiting a long time to tell his story, and finally given the chance it came out in a great burst of words. "I went down to the Plains for my mail and I stopped a little bit at Henry Smith's grocery store and was sitting there in the door and Greek came in and walked back towards where the bucket stood in the middle of the floor and then walked back again and stood in the door and the mail-boy was going along and says he, 'You're early this morning?' Says he, 'Yes, I wanted to start when it was cool and have the cool time for it.' At that he stepped off and was going up towards the post office. Hearing these words, I concluded to go up too and get my mail and I stepped out of the door and Greek was about as far from me as from me to you..."

Hitt estimated ten or twelve feet and so noted in his transcript. "...when I went out on the walk, but I am before my story. Greek halted when I came out and he heard me and I caught up with him and he says, 'John, I allow to whip Quinn Harrison today.' Says I, 'Greek, what's that all about?' He made no reply to me. Says he, 'I allow...'" Hitt tried to shake the throbbing from his hand, causing him to miss the occasional word.

"'…do it this day if I get a chance.' I says, 'You had better let that alone, Greek.' He made no reply, only walked ahead. I went up to Turley's with him and as we went he said he was expecting him in there after his mail."

"Who," Lincoln asked, "Quinn?"

"Yes."

A fundamental rule of the business of the law is that a smart lawyer gets out of the way of his witness once he gets the stone rolling downhill. So Lincoln mostly stood aside and let Allen tell his story.

"At Turley's," Dr. Allen continued, "he made a stand at the door to knock him down as he came in. He was in there a little while and the first thing I saw he pulled off his coat and his hat and laid them down beside the showcase, Mr. Turley's and stood there. But Mr. Harrison did not come in and after a few minutes he went and put his clothes on again."

"Where did he go?"

"The last I saw of him he was pulling off his coat as he walked in where the affray happened. It was not exceeding half an hour before the affray began."

"Your witness, John," Lincoln said.

Dr. Allen shifted in the witness chair, turning his body to face the prosecution's table. Palmer remained seated. He appeared to read notes scribbled on a page.

"Do you recall if Mr. Turley was in the store at the time?"

"I don't remember seeing him. It was his store, I can't say whether he was there or not." Like several other previous witnesses, Dr. Allen seemed to have adjusted his attitude while talking to opposing counsel. Rather than being free with his words, like he had been with Lincoln, he was far more guarded in his responses to Palmer's questions.

And Palmer's questions came quickly. They were short and precise. Questioning continued along this line for many minutes, going over a well-set path time and again without anything of consequence being said by Dr. Allen. Finally, Palmer thanked the witness and excused him.

23

John Purvines, Abijah Nottingham, and James S. Zane, each in turn, testified to Crafton saying he intended to harm Harrison. They recalled him saying he would, "whip," "thrash," and "stamp on him."

Palmer cross-examined each witness. Hitt wondered why the other members of the prosecution team did not relieve him from time to time. They all had fine reputations. But they did not, and truthfully John Palmer seemed none the worse for it. In fact, he seemed to be enjoying it.

Finally, all the witnesses for the defense had testified.

ABRAHAM LINCOLN PRESIDENTIAL LIBRARY AND MUSEUM

John M. Palmer, lawyer for the prosecution.

Lincoln faced the bench and announced, "Our evidence is all presented, your Honor. The defense rests."

Once again, the courtroom came to life, as if a withheld breath suddenly had been released. Judge Rice gave them a minute. Then he banged his gavel. "We're not done yet," he announced. "Mr. Palmer still has a couple of people he wants us to hear from. So quiet on down please."

Palmer thanked the judge, then began his rebuttal

case. He called Jacob Epler to the stand. The townsfolk knew and liked Epler, who ran the general store in Pleasant Plains. Throughout the years he'd extended credit to many of them, helping them get through tough times. He was also a man who stood by his word. His word was every bit as valuable as that of Peter Cartwright.

Epler told Palmer he knew both young men, and had spoken with Crafton on the day of the incident, after the cutting was done.

"Do you know when Mr. Peter Cartwright was there?"

"Yes, sir. I was not there when Mr. Cartwright was there," he said. Then after some thinking corrected himself, "Yes, I was there too, where he was there."

Palmer stopped here. He told the judge that Epler was going to testify that Greek had said some other things after the Reverend Cartwright left. And his words had not been so forgiving of Harrison.

Lincoln objected vehemently. He and Palmer argued back and forth. Each man made a good case for his position. As in many legal matters, Hitt knew, both sides in this argument had merit. It would be a close call for the judge, whichever way he decided.

Judge Rice took the same position he had held earlier. He decided to hear the testimony without the jury present. Then he would rule. The jury was led out of the room again. After they had gone, Palmer asked Epler, "State if you heard Mr. Crafton say anything about the connection of Mr. Harrison with his death, after the time Mr. Cartwright was there and held his conversation with him."

Epler had a soft voice. Several people in the gallery had to cup both ears with their hands to try to hear him better. "It was after the conversation with Mr. Cartwright," he said, referring to the first of several conversations Cartwright would have had with Greek Crafton. "But I would have to bring in about Mr. Short's coming in to make it plain."

"Yes, go on."

"Well, Mr. Short came in. That is Mr. B. J. Short that you have had before you, I presume. As he was coming in, Greek from where he lay, could see him coming through the gate and he just named him, 'If it hadn't been for that man, Mr. Short, he wouldn't have been there.'"

Epler hesitated, trying to remember Crafton's exact words. "I want to have it right," he said. "You've got me bothered. Well, I don't know that there was anything more said in regard to Harrison."

"Is that all you remember?" Palmer asked sympathetically.

This was a very important point. According to Epler, Crafton believed that Short's involvement was actually not helpful. Rather, it was an interference that had essentially caused the tragedy!

Epler was struggling. "That was all he said, I believe, to [about] Mr. Short," he finally said. "He [Greek] was asking after that whether Harrison had yet been taken by authority." Epler recalled that being important to Crafton: Had Harrison been arrested? He remembered that Crafton had asked it several times.

Both Lincoln and Logan stood up at almost the same time. They looked at each other, somewhat surprised and pleased. The judge motioned for them to sit. After all, the jury wasn't even present. So there was no need to object.

Epler finished up. "He said it was true that Harrison was taken into custody. That's all. That's the sum and substance."

Now Logan stood to make the defense's argument. He stated loudly that the jury should not hear Epler's testimony because it was not at all rebuttal testimony. It did not contradict Reverend Cartwright's recounting of the facts. Therefore, it did not belong in this portion of the trial. Epler should have testified when the prosecution made its case, Logan said. Not now.

The judge reserved his ruling on Epler for the time being. He asked Palmer to move on.

Palmer announced that the prosecution would like to recall Dr. J. L. Million. Million would testify that during all the hours he had spent at Crafton's bedside he had never heard him, in any way, forgive Peachy or put blame on himself. It made sense, Palmer said, to hear both of these witnesses before the judge made up his mind about Epler being able to testify and before the jury was recalled. The defense agreed, and Dr. Million was recalled.

Million sat straight up, almost rigid, in the chair, halfway back in the seat. Palmer asked him, "State whether you had any conversation with Greek Crafton after Mr. Cartwright had the interview, about the connection of Mr. Harrison with his death?"

"Not after," Million corrected him. "Before Mr. Cartwright had his interview."

"Did you hear him say anything about Quinn Harrison after that conversation?"

"No, sir, I don't recollect hearing him say anything after Mr. Cartwright was there."

"Did you hear him say anything about it before Peter Cartwright was there?"

"Yes."

"What was his condition at the time?"

"I would say he was rational."

When Million was done the defense objected to his testimony as well. Judge Rice pondered the situation for a few minutes. Then he pointed out that Greek Crafton's statements to Epler and Million were made *before* his remarks to Reverend Cartwright. They were made *before* he was aware his wounds were going to be fatal. As such, according to the law, they did not qualify as appropriate rebuttal. Nor were they considered a dying declaration. Therefore, he had no choice but to sustain the defense objection. Neither man would testify before the jury.

Disappointed, Palmer said he had no more evidence. He looked up at Judge Rice, spread his palms in a gesture indicating he'd finished, and said, "The prosecution rests, your Honor."

Judge Rice informed both sides that court would resume the following morning at 9:00 a.m. when closing arguments would begin. He brought the jury back into the courtroom and reminded them that they weren't to talk about the case with anyone, absolutely anyone,

"Even if she threatened she wasn't going to fix your dinner," which drew a hearty laugh. Then he wished everyone a pleasant evening and banged the proceedings closed.

24

In a closing argument all the skills of a lawyer are needed. Until this point, a trial is a battle of facts. But a closing argument is a time for a lawyer to sum up those facts and present them in a way that is most favorable to his case. A closing argument is a time for a lawyer's speech to combine intelligence and passion, to show character, and to seek justice. It is also a lawyer's final opportunity to speak directly to the jury.

Lincoln knew how to talk to a jury. He knew how to reach out and grab hold of their emotions and get jurors on his client's side. Hitt had been told repeatedly that no lawyer closed his case better than Lincoln.

As Hitt knew from his own experience, Lincoln's summation skills were not limited to emotional appeals. He was equally skilled at putting highly technical information into plain language that anyone could understand. And, of course, he did this in a way that benefitted his client.

In 1859, closing arguments were still a relatively new addition to criminal trials. They had started to be used in England in 1836. Before then, judges had done the summing up, and they often let the jurors know what verdict they wanted!

When closing arguments became a lawyer's responsibility, rules developed about what might be said. Most summations consisted of a presentation of the facts, a rebuttal of the opponent's case, and an emotional appeal to reason. Lawyers were not allowed to bring in facts not presented during the trial, misstate the testimony of witnesses, or put words in a man's mouth. Lawyers were not allowed to suggest to jurors that they follow their heart, or plead for sympathy. Nor were they permitted to draw attention to a defendant's ethnicity, race, nationality, or religion.

Except for those restrictions, a lawyer was limited in his talk only by his own imagination and his powers of persuasion. And attorneys were allowed to personally show as much emotion as they so chose. Lincoln, for example, had been known to shed tears.

A great closing argument was top-notch entertainment, liable to be talked about for days afterward. And so, everyone was expecting that Lincoln's closing argument in this case was going to be a humdinger.

Of all the days of the heat wave, this was by far the worst.

But it did not keep spectators away. When Hitt arrived at the courthouse, there was a long line outside. Inside, the courtroom was stifling. Several volunteers were busy fanning the room, trying to get the air circulating before they let people in.

Hitt would not be transcribing the closing arguments, but he would not have missed being there to hear them. Judge Rice laid down the rules as if he was overseeing a bare-knuckle fight. The prosecution would have first say. He wasn't going to put any limit on the number of lawyers who might speak or limit their time.

Norman Broadwell spoke first for the prosecution. He stood behind their table, and referred often to his notes. His part in the summation was to re-present the facts and explain how the law applied to them.

Broadwell spoke for almost an hour. He reminded

the jury what each witness had said: Greek Crafton had died slowly from knife wounds inflicted by the accused, Quinn Harrison. The dispute had begun at the town picnic on the Fourth of July, when Harrison was heard to warn his brother to stay away from the Craftons. Over the next days the two young men told friends they were preparing for a fight, although—and Broadwell emphasized this point—the defense had presented not a shred of evidence that Harrison had direct knowledge of Crafton's remarks. However, Crafton had been warned that Harrison was getting a weapon: a gun or a knife. And yet he still came to the fight completely unarmed. It was clear he intended this to be a fair fight, no different than the countless fights between spirited young men that take place every single day. It was only because of the actions of the accused, Quinn Harrison—and with that he turned dramatically and pointed at Harrison—that everyone had been brought into this sweltering courtroom.

Hitt glanced at Lincoln, who was sitting perfectly still. His head was tilted back, and his face showed no movement, no response, no emotion. His eyes were so completely fixed on a spot on the ceiling that Hitt followed his gaze upward to see what had caught his attention.

There was nothing there, of course, nothing at all.

Hitt realized this was Lincoln in full concentration. His mind was locked on Broadwell's presentation.

Broadwell was explaining that the law might not always match each person's beliefs about right and wrong. But because those beliefs varied so much—even among the wise men of this jury—the law provided a measuring stick that everyone could follow. And that law offered no protection to Harrison. The law didn't say anywhere that you could stab someone who was hitting you. What it did say is that you can use deadly force only when absolutely necessary, like when your life was in jeopardy. Throughout this entire trial, he argued, there was not even a suggestion that Quinn Harrison's own life was threatened. Even the testimony by the Reverend Cartwright did not mention any claim from Crafton that he intended to cause serious harm to Harrison. For all those reasons, Broadwell said, his voice rising, the members of the jury had no choice but to find the defendant guilty. He sat down. The courtroom was respectfully silent.

Broadwell's argument had been factual and logical. He had set a high standard. The defense had its work cut out for it.

Cullom stood to make the first statement for the defense. He stood near the jury and began by laying out the defense's version of the facts. There was bad blood between the Crafton and Harrison families. Words were spoken. Greek Crafton was pushed by his father to…

Suddenly Cullom coughed. He asked the court to bear with him. He sat and sipped some water. Then he stood up and began again. Words were spoken between Crafton and Harrison. Crafton was pushed by his father to defend the family honor. The jury had heard for themselves how many people Crafton had told he was going to stamp and maul the much smaller Harrison. He…he…

The attorney sat down again. His color was drained. He clamped his palm over his mouth to prevent an accident. The heat, perhaps along with some nervousness, had overwhelmed him. Logan quickly stood to take over. Cullom weakly thanked him and then, with some help, left the courtroom.

Later, Cullom would write about that moment: "The courthouse was crowded with people and it was hot and smoldering. I was so overcome with the heat and the great responsibility I thought was resting upon me as a young lawyer I broke down in the midst of my speech and practically had to be carried out of the courtroom."

25

Logan, as always, was completely prepared. In a thorough and utterly professional presentation he laid out in simple terms why the jury must find Harrison not guilty of murder.

Like Broadwell, Logan reviewed the facts that had been heard in the courtroom. Not surprisingly, his interpretation of those facts differed in almost every way from the prosecution's interpretation. Harrison had almost gotten into a fight with Crafton at the town picnic, but the young men had been separated before any harm was done. As the jury could plainly see just by looking at him, Harrison was small and slender, while witnesses described Crafton as having been a much larger and stronger man. In addition, Harrison had been ill for a considerable time, with an illness that had sapped his strength. He did not set out on the morning of the sixteenth to confront Crafton—he was not looking for a fight. He did not see Greek Crafton, who had lain in wait to surprise him at Turley's store and then followed him to Short's. It was there, as he was sitting peacefully reading a newspaper, that he was attacked and grabbed from behind. He did not try to fight back. Instead he held on to the rail tightly. He even called out for help. Numerous witnesses heard him scream, "Have I no friends here?" It was only after he had been pulled free, and it appeared that John Crafton might join the fray, that in fear for his life he had struck back with the only weapon he had available to him.

Greek Crafton's intentions that day were well-known. He had been telling everyone who would listen to him what he was going to do to Harrison. He was going to stamp him! He was going to maul him! He had been given permission from his father to defend the family honor. He had promised he was going to hurt Harrison, but only he knew exactly what that meant. There could be no doubt, however, as to his frame of mind when he attacked Harrison that morning. The anger that welled inside him was bursting to get out. He had put his own reputation and that of his family on the line. Anything less than giving Peachy a beating would not satisfy Greek's thirst for revenge.

At this point Logan began referring directly to the Reverend Cartwright's testimony. He had written down a few of the phrases he had used and quoted them. In his dying declaration, Crafton admitted he had started the fight and had come to regret it. But in his last moments he found extraordinary courage, and accepted responsibility for his actions. Logan gave credit to Greek for coming clean in what must have been a difficult confession.

After Logan's dramatic re-creation of Cartwright's testimony, Judge Rice decided he needed a break from the heat. He interrupted Logan and asked him to pick up again after everyone had an opportunity to cool down a little. Having already spoken for more than an hour, Logan readily agreed.

Hitt watched as Lincoln and Logan escorted Harrison to their waiting room. It occurred to him at that moment that he had never heard the sound of Harrison's voice. Harrison was the most important person in the entire trial, the very reason for the whole as-

ABRAHAM LINCOLN PRESIDENTIAL LIBRARY AND MUSEUM

During his presidency, Lincoln would describe Stephen Trigg Logan as "one of my most distinguished and most highly valued friends."

sembly, and yet, he had not been allowed to speak one word in his own defense.

This struck Hitt as odd. Hitt wondered what Peachy would say if given the opportunity. Would he claim he acted out of terror? Would he apologize? Would he say it was a terrible accident? And then, how would the jury react? Would those twelve men believe him? Or would they dismiss his words as self-serving and untrue?

Had Harrison been permitted to testify, there is no doubt the trial would have proceeded differently. It would have been his story, in his own words, that the defense would have tried to support and that the prosecution would have attacked. But the law left it to others to make the case, while the man whose life was at stake sat there silently—and mostly unnoticed.

Like so many other structures in the young nation, the legal system was slowly evolving. Hitt's own place in the courtroom, writing down the exact words so anyone at any time—even over 150 years later—could know what was said here, was itself a significant advance. Hitt never flattered himself that he was writing history. He was just doing his job, just recording the words. But having a true record, being able to look back on his transcript and know this is what was said in this courtroom on this day, added immeasurably to the confidence Americans could have in their courts.

After the break Logan resumed his closing argument. Even Cullom was back in the courtroom, sitting behind Lincoln and Logan. It appeared to Hitt that the room was even more crowded than before.

Logan began by focusing on Cartwright's testimony. Although he was barred from saying outright that the reverend was not capable of lying, even to save his kin, he cleverly worked around those restrictions to make the point. Greek Crafton had accepted responsibility for the fight. If he had forgiven the defendant, the jury must do no less.

As had Broadwell, Logan went through the applicable statutes to show that Harrison had done nothing illegal by arming himself. Logan was careful to avoid saying specifically that Harrison had knowledge of Crafton's threats. They had tried to prove it during the trial, of course, with the testimony of witnesses such as P. M. Carter and Skinny Thomas White. But they had not quite managed to do that, so Logan could not state outright that Peachy knew what Greek had threatened to do to him. But he was still able to argue that Harrison had acted in self-defense.

Logan reviewed the law regarding self-defense. The right of a man to protect himself was a fundamental principle on which this nation had been founded. Was this slender young man simply supposed to stand there and be beaten senseless by a bigger, stronger attacker? By *two* attackers? He had done everything in his power to avoid the fight. He had held on to that counter as if holding on to his life. Only after he was yanked free, with one arm being held tight by Greek Crafton, Short holding on, and John Crafton entering the fight, did Peachy reach for his knife as a last resort.

Logan finished with a plea to the jurors to put themselves in the position of young Harrison, and ask themselves: If they had been in the same situation, what would they have done? Logan had no doubt that the men of the jury—several of whom, most likely, at some time in their lives had found themselves in a similar predicament—would have fought back with everything they had. What had happened was truly a tragedy. No one could dispute that. A fine young man had lost his life in a completely unnecessary fight, but the law spoke quite clearly on this matter. For all those reasons, Logan said, the members of the jury had no choice but to find the defendant innocent.

He was sweating profusely when he sat down. He wiped his face with a dampened cloth as Lincoln and then Cullom congratulated him. Judge Rice gave the courtroom several minutes to quiet down as spectators made their opinions known to their friends.

Logan had been a good match for Broadwell. Both men had made important points with conviction.

Then, Judge Rice looked at the defense table, nodded and said, "Mr. Lincoln."

Abraham Lincoln spent a few seconds straightening the papers on the table in front of him. He took a moment. Then he stood to the full of his great height and faced the jury. And smiled.

26

Abe Lincoln had a knack for making his complete preparation look casual, from the choice of his words to the cut of his cloth. He dressed to satisfy the jury. For this occasion, he wore his almost-threadbare black frock coat, a vest, an old-fashioned stock tie, shapeless brown trousers, and handmade suspenders. His boots were dull from use, although they had been soaped clean.

He walked to the jury box and took in all twelve of them with a glance. He wished them "afternoon," and said hello to those five or six men he knew by first name. Lincoln was following the first rule of good criminal lawyering, Hitt realized as he watched. He was building a relationship with the jury. He was just Abe, their neighbor, the man who shared their values and their lives, standing here hopin' they could solve this sticky problem together.

Years earlier, Hitt knew, Lincoln had given practical advice about talking to a jury to a young man he was mentoring. That advice had been passed along and passed along until even Hitt had heard it. "Talk to the jury as though your client's fate depends on every word you utter. Forget that you have any one to fall back upon, and you will do justice to yourself and your client."

Lincoln spoke to the jury in a soft voice, often dropping the final "g" of a word. It seemed natural to him. He spoke the language of the jurors. Once, in his advice to his partner, Herndon, he had cautioned him, "Billy, don't shoot too high; aim lower and the common people will understand you. They are the ones you want to reach. The educated and refined people will understand you, anyway. If you aim too high, your idea will go over the head of the masses and hit only those who need no hitting."

To make a connection to those common people, Lincoln often began his closing arguments with a story, most of the time told at his own expense. For exam-

ABRAHAM LINCOLN PRESIDENTIAL LIBRARY AND MUSEUM

William Herndon, lawyer for the defense.

ple, he might ask the jury to bear with him because he had a lot to say, and sometimes he could be a bit forgetful. In that way, he would add, he was like the old Englishman "who was so absentminded that when he went to bed he put his clothes carefully into the bed and threw himself over the back of his chair."

When a jury responded to such a story with easy

laughter, Lincoln knew he was forming a bond with them.

It is likely, based on newspaper reports from the time and everything we know of his career, that Lincoln started this closing argument by reminding jurors what a tremendous obligation lay before them. Unlike many lawyers, he did not read from the applicable statutes or quote authorities. Instead, with a sweep of his hand, he took in the bench and the prosecution, and said, "These gentlemen will allow, or Judge Rice if need be, will explain the laws that are to be applied here." It was his intention to remind them that they were holding a life in their hands. They needed to be sharp. They needed to listen and understand every word, because one word might make all the difference in their deliberations.

Peachy Quinn Harrison lay accused of committing the worst of all crimes, murder. Murder is a legal term. It is strictly defined by the statutes. But it comes down to more than a legal definition. In order to find Quinn Harrison guilty of murder, as opposed to any lesser crime, every single juror had to be convinced that Quinn intended to seriously harm Greek Crafton rather than merely defend himself. And, Lincoln argued, there had been nothing in the prosecution's case to support that.

At the very beginning of his presentation, Lincoln stood almost with his hands locked together behind him. But as he talked, he became more animated. At first he did not use his hands to emphasize his points, but then he brought them in front of him and gradually began using them in common gestures. When making a point, he suddenly would shoot out his long forefinger, an action so completely unexpected it was impossible not to follow its line to the intended target. At those moments, Herndon said, "Every organ of his body was in motion and acted with ease, elegance, and grace."

Once in motion, Lincoln remained in motion. He moved around the courtroom but always, always, returned to a place in front of the jury. The first part of his argument was a lively recitation of the evidence and the testimony the jurors had heard. Piece by piece he picked apart the prosecution's witnesses and case. He highlighted the inconsistencies and pointed out the gaps—although he was careful never to question the truthfulness of a single witness. Lincoln rarely attacked a witness. He believed doing that would damage his relationship with the jury and the harm from that would be greater than any gain he sought.

Instead, Lincoln portrayed all witnesses as friends and neighbors. They were good people, who, of course, were telling the truth. But even good people tended to remember things different, 'specially when there was a whole hullabaloo going around them. He pointed at the diagram that had been used by both sides to try to figure out who was standing where and doing what at what point. The jurors had heard a lot of testimony about where the various players were at each point in the event, who was to the east or the west or the northeast. But—and here he scratched his head—if they could figure out for sure what was goin' on each few seconds, maybe they could explain it to him! John Crafton remembered it one way, while Short remembered it differently—and they were both in the middle of it. There was no question that both of them were trying to tell the truth, but if *they* couldn't agree on how it happened, well, how could anybody expect the jurors to sort it out? Lincoln threw his arms into the air, palms up. He had no answer to that question.

In his summation, Lincoln made a point of acknowledging the opposition's case, something neither Broadwell or Logan had done. He praised the fine work done by his old friend John Palmer. At that point he may have even mentioned, just as an aside, that there probably was no finer advocate in all of Illinois than John Palmer, a man who had trained so many fine lawyers, among them His Honor Edward Y. Rice.

Palmer had made some very strong points, Lincoln reckoned, and he wasn't about to dispute all of them. As he did in most of his cases, he reviewed the prosecution's case, and agreed with certain elements. Yes, Harrison had carried a knife. And yes, he had slashed Greek Crafton.

Lincoln continued to go through the prosecution's case and mention almost every one of their witnesses. He spoke at this point without any great display of emotion. He might have even sounded very much like a professor leading his students through an especially interesting lesson as opposed to a lawyer fighting for his client's life.

But slowly Lincoln wound his way into the core of the case. He moved step-by-step away from the facts and into his interpretation of them.

At some point in his presentation Lincoln paused to remove his coat, which he put on the back of his chair, maybe even for effect. He then began the next portion of his summation.

He finally let loose the speaking abilities that had marked him as a man whose words could spark true emotions in his listeners. This was the Abraham Lincoln the spectators had packed the courtroom to hear. His voice until this moment had been pleasing as he had lulled not just the jury, but everyone in the courtroom, into a sense of comfort. Now, with equal ease, he took them out of it.

Lincoln's voice grew louder and became colored with emotion. His words cut through the calm air he had created. Lincoln had done the legal job; now he was going for the heart.

He took off his vest, hooked his fingers in his suspenders, and began telling his stories. As he talked, one of the suspenders fell off his shoulder and hung loosely at his side. He made no move to pull it up. It was questionable he even knew it had slipped, because he was so focused on his remarks. And everyone was focused on him. This was the Lincoln that Hitt had seen on the platform with Douglas, the man with the ability to make every single person in a large crowd feel as though he was speaking directly to them.

At times like this Lincoln might talk about impulsive young men ripe with emotions, emotions that sometimes got confused and wrapped together and caused people to overcome their own good sense. He might reach back into his own younger days and begin talking about his own errors. He had been pretty good with an ax in those days. He had won several rail-splittin' contests, and there was one mighty important lesson he had learned: once a rail was split there was no putting it back together.

There was no doubt at all in his mind, Lincoln declared, that given another opportunity, these two decent young men would have found another way to settle their differences. This outcome wasn't what they had wanted. It wasn't what anyone had wanted. And a lot of people were suffering because of it. But there was no going back. That rail had been split, so to speak. The damage was done. And what was left to do was figure out how to settle things fairly.

Then he started talking about Greek Crafton. In case anyone didn't know it, Greek had trained in his office. He had intended to become a lawyer. Maybe someday he would have even stood right here defending another young man. Lincoln described Crafton, talking about his skills and the delight he took in little things. He talked about his own pain in accepting that Greek was gone, and that all the promise Greek had had would never be fulfilled.

A sob came from the gallery. It was likely from either a family member or a close friend. This was what Greek's family had craved: that someone would stand up and talk about their loss. The fact that it was the lawyer for the accused made it all the more remarkable and meaningful.

The coat that Greek Crafton had been wearing during the affray was lying on a table. Lincoln picked it up and held it open. The gash marks made by Harrison's borrowed knife were clearly visible. Lincoln shook his head sadly at this evidence of the loss. Then he laid the coat carefully on the table.

It is possible, he continued, to mourn the death of a son, a loved one, a friend, without placing blame for it on a man innocent of all murderous intent. What happened was a tragedy. To find Quinn Harrison guilty of anything other than being young and scared would do nothing but further the tragedy. Lincoln's words poured out of him without even a slight pause.

And then Hitt, who was once again captivated by Lincoln, suddenly realized why he was so deeply affected by this speech:

Lincoln meant every word of it. This wasn't a performance. It wasn't the flimsy theater he had seen other lawyers put on for a jury. This was not an attempt to manipulate emotions. Lincoln's compassion was real. The tragedy was real to him.

Lincoln's presentation went on for almost two hours. He didn't hesitate for an instant. His shirt became drenched with sweat.

Upon finishing his remarks, Lincoln paused one last time in front of Greek Crafton's slashed coat and stared at it, as if saying his final goodbye. Then he sat down and busied himself moving papers while those in that room absorbed the impact of his words. Logan reached behind Harrison and patted Lincoln on his shoulder.

27

John Palmer stood up to speak. What happened next has been a matter of debate among historians. Although some people who were in the courtroom wrote about it later, other people dismissed it as fiction. The harshness of Palmer's response to Lincoln's closing argument may be debatable, but clearly Lincoln's emotional appeal had irritated him.

As Douglas had learned in the debates—and other lawyers in other courtrooms surely had experienced as well—following a speech by Abraham Lincoln was a difficult task. Now Palmer stunned the courtroom by responding to Lincoln's summation this way. "Well, gentlemen," he said, "you have heard Mr. Lincoln. 'Honest Abe Lincoln' they call him, I believe. And I suppose you think you have heard the honest truth..."

As it became apparent that John Palmer was launching an attack on his opponent, there was not a murmur in the room.

"...or at least what Mr. Lincoln believes what he had told you to be the truth. I tell you, he believes no such thing!"

Every eye was riveted on Palmer. One of the boys sitting in the window whistled to those outside to hush. No one wanted to miss a word of this.

"...That frank, ingenuous [trusting] face of his, as you are weak enough to suppose, those looks and tones of such unsophisticated simplicity, those appeals to your minds and consciences as sworn jurors are all assumed for the occasion, gentlemen. All a mask, gentlemen. You have been listening for the last hour to an actor, who knows well how to play the role of honest seeming, for effect."

He would have continued this attack, but Lincoln finally had had enough. "Mr. Palmer!" he shouted as he stood up. Hitt noticed that Lincoln's fists were tightly clenched. Palmer was making the kind of charge that could destroy a man's career if it was to be believed. Palmer was calling him a faker. In a firm but controlled voice, Lincoln responded, "You have known me for years, and you know that not a word of that language can be applied to me."

The two men glared at each other across the room for several seconds. They had been colleagues, friends, for decades. Each of them had great respect for the other. The irony that a trial about a death that had started with an exchange of angry words had led to this was not lost on the participants. After several seconds, Palmer's shoulders drooped, and he admitted, "Yes, Mr. Lincoln, I do know it. And I take it all back."

Cullom later remembered that the two men each moved forward a few paces and shook hands, defusing an ugly moment. And as they did, the courtroom erupted into applause.

Minutes later Palmer resumed his closing argument, perhaps having successfully planted some doubt in the minds of jurors about Lincoln's emotional appeal. Lincoln clearly had touched the jury with both his reasoning and his understanding of human nature. Palmer had felt he had no choice but to cut it down. He had apologized, but the residue of his attack could not be erased from jurors' minds.

Palmer spoke for nearly three hours. His closing argument was exceptional. He had a dazzling command of the facts and the law, and he applied them to the evidence and the testimony the jurors had heard. He laid out a line of reasoning straight and easy to follow. And yet, he was still in that unfortunate position of following Abe Lincoln.

Lincoln had carried the spectators to an emotional high and held them there. The sight of him holding up the cut coat of a young man he had tutored and bemoaning the senseless loss had broken hearts. He was not the only man in that courtroom crying, and when he was done the spectators were drained. Palmer had to step in to that moment. It was too much to expect him to be able to bring them back to a similar high point. Even if it was possible, he wasn't that kind of speaker.

Hitt guessed that Palmer knew it, too, which was why he had opened his summation by trying to challenge the truth of all that raw emotion. On a factual basis his argument was the equal of Lincoln's, maybe even stronger. The laws defining self-defense might not be to every man's liking, but the jurors were not allowed to make up their own interpretation of the law. And according to the law, Palmer insisted, this was not self-defense.

As Palmer continued, the heat in the courtroom, which somehow had seemed tolerable to Hitt during Lincoln's argument, had once again become oppressive. It was so bad it caused people to lose track of Palmer's argument. He finished strong, though, recalling the words of P. M. Carter, a defense witness who had testified that he had told Greek, "If you ever attack Quinn I believe he is determined to kill you." He also reminded the jury that James S. Zane, another defense witness, had testified that Greek had told him, "he [Harrison] threatened to kill me if I jumped him."

The prosecution finished. Now it was time for the judge to give the case to the jury.

28

Judge Rice turned to the twelve men and reviewed with them what they had to do. He laid down the law carefully, avoiding any idea that he favored one side or the other. As Rice spoke, Hitt marveled that in such a brief time these twelve individuals had seemed to become one united group. Only a few days earlier several of them seemed to be reluctant participants. But now they were all sitting there, ready, some of them even eager, to take on a jury's responsibility.

Before they were sent out to deliberate, Lincoln made a motion. It seemed to him, he said, that much of the case might be narrowed down to the testimony of Silas Livergood, a prosecution witness. Livergood had seen the fight. He had heard Harrison pleading that he didn't want it. He had seen him holding on to the rail and being pulled by Short and the Crafton brothers. He had seen the cutting. Lincoln proposed that Hitt read all of Livergood's testimony to the jury before they retired.

This was a most unusual request. Hitt blushed bright red at the mention of his name, being unused to even being mentioned in a trial. Judge Rice asked Palmer how he felt about it. Palmer said he didn't have a problem with it, but he asked for a few minutes to confer with his co-counsel. When he spoke again, he said he didn't think it was a good idea at all. The prosecution was against it.

Judge Rice accepted that and turned down Lincoln's motion. At eleven minutes after four o'clock the jury filed out, and once again the courtroom relaxed. There was a lot of discussion as to the merits of the case and, while Hitt could not confirm it, he suspected more than one wager was placed on the outcome.

All the participants came together in the middle of the courtroom. There was some hand shaking, and Lincoln and Palmer stood to the side in discussion, perhaps clearing up any sour feelings.

Rather than leaving, the crowd mostly stayed put.

This was a sign that they didn't expect the jury to stay out for long. And no one wanted to miss their return.

Harrison had been taken back into custody to await the verdict. Hitt wondered what it must feel like to be him. What was it like to know that twelve men are deciding your fate, whether you will spend the remainder of your life—however long that might be—as a free man or a prisoner? Hitt didn't know Harrison at all, but if it were him, he would be terrified.

Although he did not prepare a transcription of the closing arguments, Hitt was still tasked with reporting the details to the newspapers. He began to write his notes. Very soon after that, Captain Kidd began spreading the word that the jury had reached its verdict. While juries rarely debated for long periods of time, this one had only been at it for one hour and nine minutes, an unusually brief period. Whatever their verdict, they had come to an agreement quickly.

The courtroom filled quickly, and even after it seemed to be crammed full, more people somehow managed to squeeze inside. Every inch of space was filled. Additional people gathered outside below the windows. They were waiting for one of the boys sitting inside on the windowsills to shout out the verdict.

Lincoln and Logan walked in on either side of Harrison. Hitt thought Harrison looked especially pale. His head was bowed and he stared at the ground. The prosecution team hurried in as a group. Finally, Judge Rice took the bench and asked that the jury be brought in.

As the jury filed in, everyone looked at them to see if their faces gave away the verdict. Not one of them revealed the slightest thing. When the jurors were seated, just as it is done now, the judge asked the foreman, "Has the jury reached a verdict?"

"We have, your honor," he said, handing the bailiff a folded slip of paper.

Judge Rice asked Peachy Quinn Harrison to stand. Lincoln and Logan stood with him. The judge unfolded the paper. He was not a man for drama, so he read it aloud at once. "'We, the jury, find the defendant not guilty as charged in the indictment.'"

The courtroom exploded with a mix of joy and horror! The hurrahs were far louder, however, than the jeers from some of Crafton's supporters.

Seconds later, a cheer came from outside as the news spread. Judge Rice banged his gavel again and again, trying to restore order, but few in the courtroom heeded him.

Hitt turned around in time to see Peyton Harrison hugging Lincoln. He saw tears running down the grateful father's face. Logan and Peachy were standing behind the table. Logan had one hand on Quinn's shoulder, and the two of them were having a deep conversation. The prosecution team was gathering its papers, doing busywork. Their bowed heads made it impossible to see the expressions of their faces.

Hitt made a note to himself about the verdict, which he would later attach to the transcript. "The announcement was received by the large crowd in attendance with great and long continued applause."

After several minutes the courtroom calmed down, and now Judge Rice was able to gavel it into silence. There was still work to be done. He asked Harrison to stand. Then he officially released him. He was free to go.

Harrison shook hands in turn with Lincoln, Logan, and Cullom.

Judge Rice thanked the jury for their good work, praising them for giving their time and for their patience and thoughtful deliberations. Then he released them as well. With that he congratulated all the attorneys for their fine work in representing the interests of the state and the accused. Then he looked at the gallery and said, "It's time to go home, folks," and with a single gavel blow to the sound block he officially ended the trial.

"Court is adjourned," Captain Kidd said firmly.

By the time Hitt had packed his supplies and readied to leave, the clamor had subsided. He had watched as Harrison had left the courtroom surrounded by his friends. They had all remained respectfully low-key.

Before he left, Hitt shook hands with Judge Rice, who praised his work and told him he was a welcome presence in his courtroom anytime. Then Hitt shook hands with each of the attorneys. Lincoln also thanked him and said he looked forward to working with him sometime in the future.

Hitt was at the telegraph office when it opened the following morning. Then, thanks to the miracle of rapid rail transportation, he was back in Chicago by that evening.

Within days newspapers reported the verdict. One enterprising journalist quoted a young Springfield boy named William B. Thompson, who told him, "Mr. Lincoln saved Quinn Harrison, but it was a very hard fight. We boys followed it throughout. All of us who were able climbed to the windows. The others hung around the doors of the old courthouse. We listened with most careful attention to everything Lincoln said. His argument to the jury for Quinn Harrison made a lasting impression upon us. Harrison was acquitted.

LIBRARY OF CONGRESS PRINTS AND PHOTOGRAPHS DIVISION

The telegraph machine, invented by Samuel F.B. Morse in 1844, was a quick way to communicate important information before the telephone and other electronic devices replaced it. This drawing shows it being used during the Civil War.

We boys agreed that Lincoln's speech and earnest manner did it, rather than the evidence."

Lincoln would participate in several smaller trials in the next few months before giving himself over completely to the business of running for president. None of them would have the impact or receive as much attention as the murder trial of Peachy Quinn Harrison. The last great trial of Abraham Lincoln's legal career was done.

EPILOGUE

The village of Pleasant Plains was ripped apart by the verdict. While Harrison's supporters were pleased at what they considered a just outcome, Crafton's family and friends were furious at what they believed was a terrible injustice. Subsequently, probably to satisfy them, shop owner Benjamin Short was arrested and charged with being an accessory to the murder of Greek Crafton. His actions in trying to prevent the tragedy were seen to have somehow helped Harrison in the outcome. It was a weak charge and it was dropped long before it was brought to a trial.

The tensions and even the outcome did not affect the deep friendship between Lincoln and Palmer. In fact, less than two months after the end of the trial,

Lincoln sent a note to Peachy Quinn Harrison asking him to support John Palmer in Palmer's quest to fill a seat in Congress left vacant by the death of four-term representative Thomas L. Harris. "I have no doubt that our friends are doing the best they can about the election," he wrote. "Still, you can do some more, if you will. A young man, before the enemy has learned to watch him, can do more than any other. Pitch in and try. Palmer is good and true, and deserves the best vote we can give him. If you can make your precinct 20 votes better than it was last we probably shall redeem the country. Try. Yours truly, A. Lincoln."

Perhaps Lincoln hoped Harrison might rally those friends of his still angry at the prosecutor for his work in the trial. Palmer, however, was defeated.

No matter. Within months Palmer was able to return the favor and help Lincoln secure the Republican nomination for president.

While Lincoln remained a long-shot candidate for the 1860 Republican presidential nomination, his victory in this trial contributed to his increased visibility. Freed, mostly, from the "press of business in the courts," as he described it, he began speaking throughout the Midwest, seeking to establish that region as his base to support him during the convention. He was testing the political waters, while at the same time denying interest in the presidency. He wrote to a supporter, "In regard to the matter you spoke of. I beg you will not give it further mention. Seriously, I do not think I am fit for the presidency."

Only weeks after the conclusion of the Harrison trial, Lincoln received an invitation to speak at New York City's Cooper Institute the following February. His speech there was widely reprinted in its entirety. Publisher Horace Greeley wrote in his *New York Tribune*, "No man ever made such an impression on his first appeal to a New York audience."

Lincoln had no organization, no campaign funds, and little political experience. His opposition was Senator William Seward, who had all of these things. At the Republican convention in May, John Palmer, Stephen Logan, and Judge David Davis, working together, helped secure the nomination for Lincoln. But it was another member of the prosecution team who claimed credit for it.

As a member of the Illinois delegation, which was hosting the Republican convention in Chicago, young Norman Broadwell was assigned the oft-thankless task of arranging the seating for the delegations. As he explained to his son, Rufus, he put the state delegations committed or leaning to Seward at the front, placed delegations favoring Lincoln in the center, and whenever possible, those committed to other candidates or in doubt in the rearmost seats. Seward led after the first ballot, but his supporters were separated from those in the back who had voted for a third candidate, while the Lincoln people moved easily among them. By the third ballot the Lincoln supporters had converted enough of the other delegates to vote for Lincoln. So it would appear that thanks, at least in part to Broadwell's seating chart, Lincoln won the nomination.

The following November Lincoln was elected the sixteenth president of the United States. From 1861 to 1865 he guided the nation through the Civil War. He held the country together through its worst times and cemented his position as one of America's greatest leaders.

Since then, for more than 150 years, Abraham Lincoln's life and deeds have represented the best of this nation.

Many other participants of the trial also went on to lead long and distinguished lives. John Palmer rose to the rank of brigadier general of the Union army in the Civil War. Afterward he served as military governor of Kentucky where, as promised, he drove "the last nail in the coffin" of slavery, "that abominable institution." Following the war, he was elected governor of Illinois and in 1890 was sent by that state to the US Senate.

Two years later he was considered a serious candidate for the Democratic presidential nomination. He did make a run for it in 1896, but at seventy-nine years old, he was considered too old.

The wealthy Stephen Logan offered substantial financial support to Lincoln's presidential run, then retired in 1861.

When his partner assumed the presidency, William Herndon left the sign for the law firm Lincoln and Herndon hanging outside their office—as Lincoln had requested. Herndon continued to practice law, and eventually published a long and controversial biography of Lincoln that remains in print today.

The youngest member of the defense team, Shelby Cullom, went on to have a distinguished political career. In addition to serving as governor of Illinois, he was elected to three terms in the House of Representatives and five terms as a United States senator from that state. As a senator he championed significant legislation, including the Interstate Commerce Act of 1887, which guaranteed fair treatment to all customers of America's railroads.

John Alexander McClernand, a member of the prosecution, served in the Civil War as a brigadier general. He saw action in several of the great battles of the war, including Shiloh and the siege of Vicksburg. But there was bad blood between him and General Ulysses S. Grant, which eventually caused McClernand to resign from the army.

After a long and distinguished judicial career, Judge Edward Y. Rice served as a delegate to the state constitutional convention. In 1870 he was elected to congress. He served one term and, after being defeated for reelection, returned to the practice of law.

The Reverend Peter Cartwright continued with his popular ministry, and perhaps due to Lincoln's hard work in his grandson's trial, came full circle in his appreciation of the man. At an 1862 dinner with the president's political opponents, he told them, "Once we [Lincoln and Cartwright] were opposing candidates for a seat in Congress, and, measured up in the ballot-box, I went down in defeat. But it was defeat by a gentleman and a patriot. I stand here tonight to commend to you the Christian character, sterling integrity, and far-seeing sagacity [wisdom] of the President of the United States."

Given a second chance, Peachy Quinn Harrison could never seem to find satisfaction in life. In 1867 he married Emeline LaMothe Guillet, the widow of a Confederate officer. But his hotheaded personality caused a rift, and he left her and their two children for years at a time, often disappearing into the untamed West.

Peachy made news once again in 1885, when a dispute with his sister, Sarah, over their father's missing will became violent. He called her "a ghoul" for her actions at this time of grief. When she challenged him, he pushed her backward and she fell over a couch, breaking a rib. The Springfield newspapers claimed she had been thrown violently and was near death, using the opportunity to reprise the story of Abe Lincoln's last great criminal trial. Sarah made a rapid and full recovery, while Peachy became known for the fanciful stories he told about his adventures in the Old West and the time Lincoln saved his life.

In his later years, one of the most successful participants in the trial was Robert Roberts Hitt, the court stenographer. As was noted in the *Congressional Record* honoring his long service, "All during the Civil War and later, Mr. Hitt was employed in many confidential capacities and his abilities and proficiencies [skills] were so well recognized that his services were constantly sought by commissions, by committees of Congress, by military courts and by the Executive departments."

After the end of that war, Hitt accompanied General Grant on a notable world tour. In 1874 President Grant appointed him first secretary of the American legation in Paris, during which time he also served as Chargé d'Affaires. Returning to this country, Hitt was appointed assistant secretary of state under James G. Blaine during the administrations of President James A. Garfield and President Chester A. Arthur. He was elected to the first of his twelve terms in Congress in 1882, eventually becoming chairman of the Committee on Foreign Affairs.

He served as regent of the Smithsonian Institution and was elected a member of the National Geographic Society. In 1906 he was mentioned as a possible candidate for the vice presidency, but he died in September of that year.

At some point Hitt's original transcript of the Harrison trial was bound with a ribbon and put aside. It was discovered in 1989 in a shoebox stored in a garage of a Fresno, California, home once owned by Peachy Quinn Harrison's great-grandson. And from that transcript so perfectly stored over the years, we have the final direct link to the last great trial of Abraham Lincoln's legal career—an event that helped propel him to the presidency.

★★★★★

GLOSSARY

abolitionist: A person who wants to put an end to slavery

accessory: A person who knowingly contributes to a crime

acquittal: Setting someone free from legal charges

admissible: Permitted in a court of law

adversary: A person on the other side of an issue

alleged: Supposed but not yet proved

appeal: A closed case reviewed by a higher court when there is a desire to change the decision that was made

attorney: Lawyer

bailiff: A court officer

citation: A quote

contempt of court: Being rude or disrespectful to a judge or others in a courtroom

cross-examination: The questioning of a witness by lawyers for the other side

defense: In a court of law, the side of a person being accused of a crime

deliberate: To think about and discuss a case and decide on an outcome

deliberations: The discussion of a case by a jury to decide on an outcome

duodenum: The first section of the small intestine

foreman: The leader of a jury

gavel: A small hammer-like object used by a judge to quiet down a courtroom

hearsay: Secondhand information

homicide: Murder

imminent: About to occur

impartial: Open-minded

indict: To formally charge someone with a crime

indictment: The formal charge against someone accused of a crime

jury panel: A group of people from which jurors will be selected

legislature: A group of lawmakers

manslaughter: A killing that was not planned beforehand

mistrial: A trial that doesn't continue because the judge decides it cannot, for whatever reason

motions: Proposals made to a judge

overrule: To rule against a lawyer's argument

precedents: Similar things that happened before

presiding: In charge

presume: To believe to be true

proceedings: Legal action

prosecution: In a court of law, the side trying to prove someone guilty of a crime

rebuttal: Disproof

reconvene: To gather again

refute: To prove wrong

statute: A law

subpoena: To summon someone to testify in court

summation: Closing argument in court

summons: An order to appear in court

sustain: To allow

telegraph: A machine that allows for electronic long-distance communication

testimony: Things said under oath in a courtroom

Underground Railroad: A system created to secretly help get slaves to places where they could be free

verdict: A decision

ACKNOWLEDGMENTS

First and foremost I would like to thank my co-author, David Fisher. David is not only an incredibly gifted writer but he approached this project with a laser focus on, and appreciation for, historical detail that helped tell the story surrounding the trial. After all, when one ventures to chronicle anything Lincoln related, you best be prepared to present something beyond the hundreds of deeply researched accounts that already exist. Thanks to David, we were able to bring to life even the more obscure characters as well as Springfield, Illinois, in the year before it would become defined by the sixteenth president. The recurring question I would send as we exchanged notes: "How do we know this to be true?" Each and every time he would send back a historical reference or proof that unquestionably supported the contention. I must admit that I was thoroughly impressed when he was able to present a picture of Captain T. S. Kidd, the court crier, to back up his physical description.

I should also note that David brought this potential partnership to me along with his talented literary agent, Frank Weimann. David and I did not know one another before this project and a collaboration such as this can end up being fraught with potential personal or professional mines. We encountered none. At each milestone in the process, David overdelivered and I feel truly lucky to have him as my partner in this and a future endeavor.

I also want to thank Peter Joseph from Hanover Square Press, who was willing to bet on this as one of his first releases with a new imprint. His notes and feedback were always helpful and on point. Simply put, his intellect and appreciation for the subject matter just made the book better. Many thanks also to Thea Feldman.

My sister, Ronnie, a federal judge, and her husband, Greg, always serve as models of rectitude [integrity] in the law and beyond for me and I'm convinced Lincoln would have admired both of them for it. I have long been so proud of their insightful daughters, Dylan, Teddy, and Finn, who are always available to offer me more than a dollop of humility.

No one has unequivocally supported me in the myriad of sometimes surprising life and professional choices more than my loving mother (*eema*), Efrat, who helped shape the person I am today.

My father, Floyd, to whom this book is dedicated, remains the most trusted advisor in my life. On anything from an opinion article I am contemplating, to a house I am buying, to a legal issue I am analyzing, to this book, I always run it by Dad for his thoughts first. I recall as a teen asking how I might become a better writer, like him. "There is only one way," he responded. "Read more books." While I am not certain I heeded the advice immediately, those words continue to inspire.

Finally I want to thank the phenomenal woman I have been lucky enough to partner with on my most important project. Thank you, Florinka, for bringing our child into the world with me and for surpassing even the unreasonable hopes and dreams I had for you as a mother. I am truly blessed to have you in my life. Everything else pales in comparison to the love I have for my beautiful son, Everett. Becoming a parent, of course, changes everything.

—*Dan Abrams*

I would like to begin by acknowledging our publisher, Peter Joseph; it has been my great pleasure watching his professional success and Dan Abrams and I are thrilled to be part of his first list. I also want to thank Dan, who has been the complete collaborator, contributing to every aspect of this book with his creativity, curiosity, intelligence, and insistence on meeting and maintaining the highest standards. He pushed and pulled in all the right places and did so with absolute professionalism. I also appreciate the efforts of Fred Rappoport, who brought us together, and our agent, Frank Weimann of Folio, who always has my back.

Dan and I would also like to thank Maureen Wilburn, whose research concerning her family, the Harrisons, has proved invaluable.

We urge interested readers to visit www.ourbigfamilyhistory.com for the 330-year story of survival, endurance, and love of family and country.

We would also like to thank Donna Aschenbrenner of Donna's House of Type, Inc. of Springfield, Illinois, for supplying the Lloyd Ostendorf Images, and Curtis Mann, Sangamon Valley Collection Manager at the Lincoln Library.

I was very fortunate at Syracuse University to have been a student of the late Dr. Michael Sawyer, whose love of constitutional law was infectious and who played an important role in my life. And then I had the privilege of working with Johnnie Cochran, who never stopped loving the possibilities of our legal system.

My brother and sister-in-law, Richard and Elise Langsam, and my nephew Andrew Glenn are all attorneys and represent the best of that profession. I also have several friends, lawyers all, whom I greatly admire. These include the inimitable Captain Arthur Perschetz; George Zelma, whose impact on my entire family will never be forgotten; Arthur Aidala, who is always there on the other end of the phone when needed; Saul Wolfe and the twins, David and Jon, who fight to make this profession better; Paul Reichler, who has spent his life using international law to fight for a better life for people around the world; Mike Vecchione, who has fought all the legal wars with tremendous integrity; David Stein, who has used the law to protect the rights of working Americans; Keith Stein, a friend of both Dan and mine; my neighbors Victor Kovner, Marty Shaw and the late Professor Jerry Leitner, and the kite-flying Jon Lindsey, who moves all the pieces on the board with such joy and skill. I want to make a special mention of the late Judge Stanley Sklar, whose love for the law was so complete that on the morning of 9/11, while New Yorkers were fleeing north from

Ground Zero, Stanley was going south, into the chaos, believing there might be a need for a judge.

My friend Brian McLane is not a lawyer, but he has spent his life skillfully using the law to make life better and easier for those people who need it most. Brian has never hesitated to go after the most powerful people on behalf of the less powerful, and most often has succeeded. On the list of people I most admire, you will find his name at the top.

I also want to offer my gratitude to James M. Cornelius, PhD, the curator of the Lincoln Collection at the Abraham Lincoln Presidential Library and Museum. From the very beginning of this project he has offered his support and guidance and his continued support is greatly appreciated.

Finally, I am so fortunate to have a partner who somehow manages to find the right words and gestures at the right time, every time. My wife, Laura, makes my life immeasurably better every day. As I often tell her, I am a very lucky man to have met her, and that she chose me.

—*David Fisher*